Iroquis Foods and Food Preparation

BY

F. W. Waugh

University Press of the Pacific
Honolulu, Hawaii

Iroquois Foods and Food Preparation

by
F. W. Waugh

ISBN: 1-4102-0776-5

Copyright © 2003 by University Press of the Pacific

Reprinted from the 1916 edition

University Press of the Pacific
Honolulu, Hawaii
http://www.universitypressofthepacific.com

In order to make original editions of historical works available to scholars at an economical price, this facsimile of the original edition of 1916 is reproduced from the best available copy and has been digitally enhanced to improve legibility, but the text remains unaltered to retain historical authenticity.

CONTENTS.

11

ILLUSTRATIONS.

Iroquois Foods and Food Preparation.

INTRODUCTION.

Iroquois foods and the customs connected therewith have been the subjects from time to time of ethnological investigation. In most instances, however, such investigations have been concerned with special phases or divisions of the subject, so that a comprehensive treatment of the subject would seem useful. The idea of the author has been, for the greater part, to deal with present-day Iroquois customs, or with those which have been practised within the memory of the older people now living on the reservations, making such references to the literature and archæology of the subject as may be required to form a connected account.

Among the more recent papers or monographs to which the writer wishes to acknowledge his indebtedness are the bulletin by A. C. Parker on "Iroquois uses of maize and other food plants" and M. R. Harrington's "Some Seneca corn foods and their preparation." Of these, the bulletin by Parker is somewhat the more comprehensive. Both are interesting and cover the field more or less thoroughly, with perhaps special reference to the New York State Iroquois.

In extenuation of having gone over some of the ground already covered by previous workers the author wishes to state that this was necessitated in the making of more extensive and intensive inquiries into practically all divisions of the subject, as well as in the fixing of a starting-point for a number of additional topics. There is also to be considered the value of corroborative evidence as to distribution and other facts connected with the customs involved.

The subject matter as a whole is the result of personal investigations conducted by the writer during the years 1912-1915 among the Iroquois of Ontario, Quebec, and New York state, covering a total of about twelve months' research, and will form one of a series in which as thorough a review as possible will be made of Iroquois material culture generally.

Among the principal informants interviewed were: Chief John Gibson (Sen.) and wife (Ca.), Chief David Skye (On.), Chief David Key (Sen.), John Echo (On.), Peter John (On.) and wife (Mo.), Thomas Key (On.), John Jamieson, jun. (Ca.), Chief David Jack (Ca.), Jake Hess (Ca.), Levi John, Simon Bumberry, Seth Newhouse, and P. J. Atkins (Mo.), Jim Daluki (a negro living among the lower Cayuga, and formerly with the Oneida), of the Grand River reservation, Brant county, Ontario; Mrs. John Williams, Paul Jacobs, and Mr. Stacey, Caughnawaga, Quebec; Barber Black, Alexander Snider, and Peter Sundown, Seneca reservation, Tonawanda, N.Y.; Baptist Thomas, Mr. and Mrs. Jairus Pierce, Onondaga Castle, N.Y.; Mrs. David Williams, Anthony Day, Henry Danford, Jacob Schuyler, Noah Homer, and others, Oneidatown, Ontario.

The linguistic data given have been decided very largely by the dialect spoken by informants. A more detailed analysis of terms, in some instances, while desirable, has of necessity been left for more specialized workers in linguistics.

PHONETIC KEY.

Vowels:

ä, as in hat.
á, a sound intermediate between the preceding and the next.
a, as in father.
α, as in but.
e, as in they.
ε, as in then.
i, as in French pique.
ι, as in pick.
o, as in note.
ɔ, slightly shorter than preceding; lips somewhat farther apart.
ω, as in law.
u, as in rule.
υ, as in pull.
ai, as in aisle.
au, like ou in out.
Superior vowel, indicates slightly pronounced vowel.

Consonants:

d, sonant or intermediate dental stop.
t. as in touch.

g, sonant or intermediate palatal stop.
k, as in kick.
dj, as *j* in judge.
tc, as ch in church.
s, as in sauce.
c, like *sh* in shall.
z, as in zones.
w, as in wish.
y, as in you.
n, as in nun.
ŋ, palatalized n as in sing.
l, related genetically in Oneida to Mohawk r; pronounced as in lull.
r, found in Mohawk; slightly trilled.
ʻ, *h*, aspirants.
ʼ, glottal stop.
Whispered syllables indicated by small caps.

Diacritical Marks:
ʻ, nasalized vowel.
ʼ, main stress.
ˋ, secondary stress.
., indicates diæresis between vowels.
·, inverted period following indicates a long vowel.
ˇ, semicircular mark following indicates a short vowel.

Abbreviations used are:
Ca., Cayuga.
Mo., Mohawk.
On., Onondaga.
Oneida.
Sen., Seneca.

AGRICULTURAL METHODS AND CUSTOMS.

THE IROQUOIS AS HORTICULTURISTS.

One of the outstanding features of Iroquois material culture was their aptitude for agriculture. This was at first concerned largely with the cultivation of corn, beans, and squashes. The importance attached to these may be noted from the fact that they were called the Three Sisters, aⁿsę na'degǫdäʻnǫ'dää' (On.) and were included among those beings to whom religious ceremonials were addressed.

A few other products, such as sunflowers and artichokes, were cultivated sparingly, also a native tobacco, the *Nicotiana rustica*, which was used for smoking and for ceremonial purposes. All of the products enumerated, with the exception of the last, were welcomed as additions to agriculture, while the various grains, vegetables, and fruits known to the Europeans were, in their turn, quickly taken up by the Iroquois.

The large fields and clearings of the latter were the admiration of early writers and explorers and they are everywhere admitted to have been the leaders in agriculture within the more northerly and easterly portion of their habitat, and to have contributed not a little to its extension among those of their Algonkin neighbours whose country was suitable for the purpose.

The evident antiquity of corn culture among the Iroquois and their position as carriers and introducers of agriculture among the various tribes to the north and northeast seem to be indicative of southern or southwestern relationships and are inconsistent with the theory of an original Iroquoian migration from another direction.

So important, in fact, were Iroquois agricultural activities that, at a later date, when it was desired to punish them effectively, this was done by annihilating their granaries and cornfields.

Among the more important expeditions of this kind was that of Denonville, who, in 1687, destroyed an immense amount of corn, including the standing crops of four villages, a work of destruction which is said to have taken seven days to accomplish. In 1696 Frontenac, who invaded the Onondaga country, spent three days destroying growing corn, which extended from a league and a half to two leagues from the fort. The expedition of General Sullivan, in 1779, furnishes many interesting items.[1] It is stated that, at Chemung, an Indian village of forty houses on the Tioga, a cornfield of sixty acres was destroyed. Around the great village of "Chinesee Castle" there were cornfields of "not less than two hundred acres, the whole of which was pulled up and piled in large heaps . . and consumed to ashes." There were seventy dwellings at this point,

---

[1] Norton, A. T., *History of Sullivan's Campaign*, p. 95.

besides a similar number of outhouses or granaries. We also find it reported that forty Indian villages, beside many scattering houses, were burned. The quantity of corn destroyed was said to have amounted to 160,000 bushels, with a vast amount of vegetables of every kind. Among the European importations noted were beets, carrots, onions, peas, turnips, cabbages, parsnips, and many others, also such fruits as the apple and the peach, which had been introduced by the missionaries. The houses possessed by the Indians at this time were described as being compact and well-built.

CORN CULTURE IN EASTERN NORTH AMERICA.

Corn culture was evidently subject to fluctuation. Champlain, for instance, found that some of the eastern Algonkins had discontinued it owing to incursions by other tribes.[1] Agriculture was practised, to some extent at least, in the Maritime Provinces, as Verazzani refers to the savages towards "Penobscot Bay and Newfoundland" as "ruder and less agricultural.[2]" The Abenaki, farther south, depended largely upon corn.[3] Along the north shore of the St. Lawrence, Iroquois settlements and cornfields were discovered by Cartier in 1534. At Champlain's visit, some seventy or more years later, these had disappeared, the region being occupied by Montagnais and other non-agricultural tribes. The Etechemin, or Malecite, were also non-agricultural,[4] as were the Algonkins of northern Ontario and of Quebec as a whole. That some of these began later to adopt agriculture is shown by the fact that upon one of Champlain's later visits, the inhabitants of Allumette island were found raising a little Indian corn,[5] as were also those living along French river and Georgian bay. The Nipissings of this region were said to cultivate the land very slightly.[6] The Saul-

---

[1] Champlain, *Voyages*, Prince Soc. ed., vol. II, p. 60.
[2] Hakluyt, *Voyages*, vol. I, pp. 70, 71.
[3] Champlain, *Voyages*, Prince Soc. ed., vol. III, p. 296.
[4] Ibid., vol. II, p. 196.
Jesuit Relations, R. G. Thwaites ed., vol. IV, p. 195.
[5] Champlain, *Voyages*, vol. I, p. 300.
[6] Ibid., vol. III, p. 114.

teurs or Sauteurs, living near Sault Ste. Marie, were non-cultivators.[1] The progress of the Montagnais is shown in the fact that, in 1634, they were raising sufficient quantities of "cereals and Indian corn" to trade with other nations.[2]

The Hurons, who are related racially to the Iroquois, cultivated corn on a large scale and, besides supplying their own wants, exchanged it for furs and other commodities with neighbouring peoples. The Huron country, in fact, was said to be "the granary of most of the Algonkins."[3] The Petuns, or Tionnontati (also Iroquois) and the Cheveux Rélevées, or Ottawas, were both found by Champlain cultivating corn and tobacco.[4]

All the nations encountered on the shores of Lake Michigan possessed fields of corn, squashes, beans, and tobacco.[5] Charlevoix remarks that "the Outaouais," who had retired to an island near the entrance to the lake, "sow here Maiz, and they have learnt this good custom from the Hurons, with whom they have lived a long time in these parts."[6] This was the last point at which such provisions could be obtained in journeying to the country of the Crees, Assiniboins, Sioux, and others to the north and west.[7]

COMMUNAL CUSTOMS.

The fields were evidently grouped more or less closely about the villages, and varied from ten or twenty to several hundred acres, according to the size of the community. Portions of these are said to have been at times reserved for general purposes, such as the provision of food for councils and ceremonies.

Sagard remarks, regarding the Hurons, that "their custom is that each household lives upon what it obtains from fishing, hunting, and planting, having as much ground as may be necessary,

---

[1] Hennepin, A New Discovery, R. G. Thwaites ed., vol. I, p. 117.
[2] Jesuit Relations, R. G. Thwaites ed.
[3] Ibid., vol. VIII, p. 115.
[4] Champlain, Voyages, vol. I, p. 303.
[5] Jesuit Relations, R. G. Thwaites ed., vol. LIV, p. 207.
[6] Charlevoix, A Voyage to North America, vol. II, p. 36.
[7] Henry, Alex., Travels and Adventures in Canada (1760-1776), pp. 48, 49.

for all the forests, plains, and uncleared ground are common to all,
and it is permitted to each one to clear and sow as much as he
wishes, is able to, or requires; and the ground thus cleared remains each person's property as long as he continues to cultivate
and to use it, though when it is entirely abandoned by its pos-
sessor, any who wishes may then take possession of it, but under no
other circumstances."[1] In one of the Relations we find it stated
that they "possess hardly anything except in common. A
whole village must be without corn, before any individual can
be obliged to endure privation."[2] This custom apparently
had its drawbacks and sometimes proved a discouragement
to industry.[3]

MAKING THE CLEARING.

The first step towards organized agriculture was naturally
the clearing of a place in which to plant the corn and other
products. This involved the removal of the trees, which was
accomplished either by felling, or by girdling them, usually in the
spring, burning away what material could be removed in this
way and finally uprooting the partly burned and rotted trunks.

Large tracts of land, as in the prairie regions, were frequently burned over to furnish clearings for fields and villages.
The explorer Galinée, in 1669, on his way to the west by way of
the Seneca country, found, between the lake and the largest
village to the east, beautiful broad meadows, on which the grass

---

[1] Sagard, *Voyage*, pt. I, p. 91.

[2] *Jesuit Relations*, R. G. Thwaites ed., vol. XLIII, p. 271.

[3] Loskiel, *History of Mission*, pt. I, p. 68: "They preserve their crops in
round holes, dug in the earth at some distance from their houses, lined and
covered with dry leaves or grass. They commonly keep the situation of these
magazines very secret, knowing that if they are found out, they must supply
the wants of every needy neighbour as long as anything is left. These may
occasion a famine, for some are so lazy that they will not plant at all, knowing
that the more industrious cannot refuse to divide their store with them. The
industrious, therefore, not being able to enjoy more from their labour than the
idle, by degrees contract their plantations. If the winter happens to be severe, and the snow prevents them from hunting, a general famine ensues, by
which many die. They are then driven by hunger to dress and eat roots of
grass or the inner bark of trees, especially of young oaks."

grew as tall as himself. In the spots where there were woods, were oak plains, so open that one could easily ride through them on horseback. This open country, he was informed, continued eastward more than a hundred leagues. Westward and southward it also extended a great distance. "Treeless meadows, more than a hundred leagues in length" were reported from the south, where great quantities of corn and fruit were grown.[1]

Trees were also felled to furnish material for dug-outs, household utensils, and other articles. A method described by David Jack was to tie some saplings around the tree, forming a small, scaffold-like structure. Sods were placed on this, water was poured over them, and a fire built up below. By alternately hacking with stone axes and burning, the tree was finally cut through. If it was desired to cut it into lengths, a double pile of sods was made around the trunk where it was to be divided, and fire applied to the space between. Chief Gibson's description of tree-felling was essentially the same, except that, according to him, a quantity of rags was tied to the end of a pole and used for wetting the trunk and localizing the action of the fire. Both Lafitau[2] and Kalm[3] give similar descriptions, indicating the method to have been one in common use.

DIVISION OF LABOUR.

"It was the men all over America," according to Lafitau, "who picked out the new sites for the villages and who cut down the heavy timbers, as the women were incapable of doing this successfully, so that the latter had only the labour of splitting or breaking it up and carrying it away."[4] Among certain eastern woodland tribes the lot of the women was evidently most severe. Jouvency, who refers perhaps more particularly to the Algonkins, states that "the care of household affairs and whatever work there may be in the family, are placed upon the women. They build and repair wigwams, carry water and wood,

---

[1] Coyne, Jas. H., *Galinée's Narrative*, Ont., Hist. Soc., 1903, p. 25.
[2] Lafitau, *Moeurs des Sauvages Ameriquain*, pt. II, p. 110.
[3] Kalm, *Travels*, vol. II, p. 38.
[4] Lafitau, *Moeurs*, pt. II, p. 109.

prepare the food; their duties and positions are those of slaves, laborers and beasts of burden. The pursuits of hunting and war belong to the men." The writer continues by pointing out that under such conditions it was impossible to bring forth fully-developed children, or to nourish them properly after they were born. Abortions were frequent and infant mortality such that hardly one in thirty survived.[1] Adair writes of the Muskhogean tribes, close neighbours of the Cherokee and Tuscarora, that "the women are the chief, if not the only manufacturers; the men judge that if they perform that office, it would exceedingly depreciate them."

Carr refers to the Iroquois as the only people among whom "it cannot be shown that the warriors did take some part either in clearing the ground or in cultivating the crop; and we find that even among them the work was not left exclusively to the women, but that it was shared by the children and the old men, as well as the slaves, of whom they seem to have had a goodly number." He also mentions the almost constant occupation of the men in hunting and fighting. He elsewhere remarks of the Indians of this area in general that "whilst, as a fact, the women, children, old men, and slaves always cultivated the fields, yet the warriors cleared the ground and, when not engaged in war or hunting, aided in working and harvesting the crop, though the amount of such assistance varied, being greater among the tribes south of the Ohio, and less among the Iroquois or Six Nations."[2]

Frequent mention is made in the Relations of the employment by the Iroquois of women to carry burdens upon their various expeditions.[3]

Mary Jemison, a white woman who lived among the Iroquois, after describing the duties which fell to the women, remarks that "their task is probably not harder than that of

---

[1] *Jesuit Relations*, R. G. Thwaites ed., vol. I, p. 257.

[2] Carr, *Mounds of the Mississippi Valley*, Smithsonian Report, 1891, p. 533.

[3] *Jesuit Relations*, R. G. Thwaites ed., vol. XLIV, p. 31.

white women" and "their cares certainly are not half so numerous, nor as great."[1]

Sagard notes briefly of the Hurons, a related tribe, that "the women are more industrious than the men, though not forced to labour."[2]

Both hunting and warfare were arduous, and from the formation of the confederacy, at least, down to comparatively recent times, the maintenance of their national existence allowed of few other occupations. With the removal of the necessity for war, the men began to assist more and more. At Onondaga Castle, however, some sixty or more years ago, it was still considered beneath a man to engage in farm work,[3] although a Brant County Onondaga states that corn-planting was not considered especially a woman's job in this locality.[4]

A growing idea of specialization in men's employments is recognizable. A man, for instance, who through physical inability was an indifferent hunter, might employ himself in the making of such articles as bows and arrows, wooden utensils, or in silversmithing and other handicrafts. The idea that these occupations were derogatory seems to have gradually disappeared.[5]

CO-OPERATIVE CUSTOMS.

The custom of mutual assistance is a very common one at present, though the prevailing idea seems to be sociability, or the principle that "many hands make light labour." "Bees" are frequent both in planting and harvesting, the women figuring prominently.

There is also an organized society for mutual aid for those requiring it through age or sickness. This belongs essentially to the more conservative element, and is noted by A. C. Parker under the Seneca name of Gai'wiu Qdànnide'oshä, "In the good

---

[1] Caswell, H. S., *Our Life Among the Iroquois*, pp. 238, 239.
Seaver, *Life of Mary Jemison*, p. 43.
[2] Sagard, Voyages, pt. I, pp. 90, 91.
[3] Information by John Echo.
[4] Information by Jairus Pierce.
[5] Williams, Roger, *Key*, p. 128.
Brickell, *Nat. Hist. of N. Carolina*, p. 364.

rule they assist one another." A woman is chosen leader of the Seneca society.[1] Chief Gibson's version of the custom was to the effect that those who wished assistance should notify the leader. The Onondaga name of the society is Adänidää᷎ sää' (charity society). Help may in this manner be furnished throughout the season. The members of the society are next notified. The membership may consist of both old and young, and each must take his own hoe or other implement along. A man and woman are appointed leaders. When the members arrive they start to work. The person inviting them must furnish corn soup. When they get through, they go into the house. The leader on the male side makes a speech congratulating the others for their kindness in assisting, and informs them that soup has been prepared.

Any one, whether rich or poor, may invite the society and "bees" may be called for husking and braiding, as well as for hoeing and planting. The Onondaga term for a husking bee is hadinu yǫ dą, or gahwe᷎noni᷎ hadinoyo' nda'nɩ'.

These customs of co-operation for social or charitable purposes were evidently quite widely adopted and practised. Roger Williams found the New England Algonkins, men and women, to the number of forty, fifty, or a hundred, joining to cultivate their fields and to build their forts. Seaver's "Life of Mary Jemison" mentions that the Iroquois women of the locality joined forces not only to expedite their work, but to enjoy each other's company. One of the older women was chosen as overseer, which was looked upon as an honour. When the time for planting had arrived, the women assembled in the morning and each one planted a row. When this was completed, she 'went to another field and planted a row, and so on until all the fields had been visited, when she would begin again in the first field.[2] Local customs of this description varied slightly from village to village, or among the various nations of the Iroquois, but the underlying principle was the same. A Brant County informant[3] states that some forty-five or fifty years ago he fre-

---

[1] Parker, A. C., *Iroquois Uses of Maize and other Food Plants*, p. 30.
[2] Seaver, *Life of Mary Jemison*, pp. 168, 169. Cf. also Adair, p. 407.
[3] Peter John, Onondaga.

quently attended bees, taking his own hoe, spoon, and pail, the latter for receiving his share of corn soup, which was prepared in the field over an open fire. When no corn was available they made doughnuts of wheat flour and fried these in grease in a frying-pan. The name applied was gahä‸gwage‸ida′wɩ‵, or "cake in the grease fried." Each worker was entitled to a cake for each row hoed or planted. When one person's corn-patch was finished they would go on to the next. When corn bread was to be baked in the ashes, or other cookery of the sort performed, the ashes and cinders were carried from one place to another, so as to provide a suitable bed for the purpose.

THE QTǫ‵WI‸Zɑs (ON., ALL THE FEMALES).

This society, which is evidently of considerable importance in planting-time ceremonies, is described by A. C. Parker under the Seneca name of Towii′sas or Sisters of the Dio‵he‸′ko. These are described as using the "land-tortoise" shell rattle, and giving thanks to the spirits of the corn, beans, and squashes (Dio‵he‸′ko meaning "these sustain our lives").[1]

Baptist Thomas, ex-chief, Onondaga Castle, stated that the purpose of the society there is "to help when a person feels sick." Any kind of rattle is used at this place. The local name given to the society is Gǫtǫwi′zɑs.

Chief Gibson, who was well-known as an exponent of the Handsome Lake doctrine, gives the following description of the society as found in his locality (the names are in Onondaga): A meeting of the Qtǫ‵ʒwi‸‵zɑs, or woman's society, is held in the spring, about a week before planting. The whole community is called or notified. A speaker is next appointed, and when the people have assembled in the longhouse (Plates II and III), he makes a speech to the effect that a good number of people still have the privilege to plant again. He gives thanks to the corn, makes an offering of oyɛ‵gwaǫ′wɩ‵, or native tobacco, and continues at some length to thank all green things, or whatever grows on earth in spring. Tobacco is used to "speak direct to the Great Mother (Eti‵nuha′′s‵ų′)." The speaker

---

[1] Parker, A. C., New York State Museum Bulletin, 144, p. 27.

may, according to Chief Gibson, conclude as follows: "Thank to our Father who art in heaven. We still have the duty an privilege of planting corn, beans, squashes, and other vegetable We ask you, our Father, to supply us this season with food, to send the game birds and animals, as usual. We thank you to-day as we have the privilege of performing our ceremony."

Two singers are now selected for the Feather Dance, in which all take part, and in this way give thanks to the four angels and the Great Spirit. When through with the dance, the next feature is the game of bowl, the women on one side and the men on the other. The articles wagered are all some kind of seeds, such as corn, beans, the seeds of the squash, pumpkin, water-melon, cucumber, musk-melon, etc. A woman is appointed to collect from the men. The contributions are placed in the centre of the longhouse. The men and women each select a player. When a player is unlucky in shaking, another player takes his or her place, and so on, until the counters are all won. The losing side appoints a speaker to congratulate the winners. The winning of the game by the women is considered more auspicious of a good harvest than success by the men. Thanks are again given to the Great Spirit (Haweni'yu')[1] at the end of the game. The speaker on the losing side says: "Now you have succeeded and we produce these seeds to your hand." A female, one of the Qtǫwiⁿzɑs, on behalf of her side then says: "My sons, we have to perform our duty in thanking our Great Three Sisters (Aⁿ sę Na'degǫdą̈'nǫ'dää'). We have now to ayagwatǫ-wiⁿsa' (sing for our Great Three Sisters), and you must help us sing." All stand up, the men lining up on one side of the centre, the women on the other. The leader of the women uses the rattle and sings, all joining in. She then says: "I have finished thank-ing our Mother," then hands the rattle to the next in line, who says, as before: "I have to sing to thank our Mother," and so on with the others. When the women have finished, their leader hands the rattle to the head man and says: "Now, my sons, it's your duty as well to sing, thanking our Great Sisters." The leading man then sings and finishes by returning the rattle

---

[1] Prayer to Great Spirit, Morgan, *League of the Iroquois*, vol. I., p. 210.

to the leader of the women, who says: "We thank our son for giving assistance," after which the men sit down.[1] The leading woman picks up a bundle of cobs of corn, or some seeds, and begins to sing walking along, followed by the rest of the women, also singing and carrying seeds. They go around about three times. The leader then says: "We have got through thanking our Sisters or Mother."[2] Then, one of those appointed to collect opens a bundle and gives the seeds to the winning side in the game of bowl. Some prominent person, such as a chief, is appointed speaker, and congratulates the people on being present and calls the attention of the women to the arrival of the season for planting.

IMPLEMENTS EMPLOYED.

Both hoeing and digging implements were employed by eastern woodland tribes. Sagard, in describing the agriculture of the Hurons, remarks that "every year they sow their corn in the same fields and places, which they freshen or renew with their little wooden shovels, made like an ear in shape, with a handle at the end; the rest of the ground is not cultivated, but merely cleared of injurious weeds.[3] Roger Williams mentions hoes of wood, while Peter Kalm speaks of turning up the ground with crooked or sharp branches. Champlain noted spade-like instruments of hardwood among the Almouchiquois and more southerly tribes.[4] Loskiel records the use of the shoulder-blade of a deer, or a tortoise shell, sharpened on a stone and attached to a stick, as a hoe.[5] "Pick-axes of wood" were observed by Hennepin. Hoes of a flat piece of antler have been frequently found on

---

[1] It was stated by John Jamieson, jun., Grand River reserve, that in the ceremonies of this kind which he had observed, the women and men sing alternately. When the men sing the women clap hands to keep time. Singing by the men is called hadowä́dä' (On.). The men do not use the rattle, which used often to be made of a mud-turtle shell painted black and spotted with red. The name he gave for the society was yundagǫ́·wi·'sa' (On.).

[2] Cf. Invocation to Pigmies at Planting Time: Parker, A. C., N. Y. State Museum Bulletin, 144, p. 27. This is not practised at Grand River.

[3] Sagard, Voyage, Tross ed., pt. I, pp. 93, 92.

[4] Champlain, Voyages, pt. I, p. 65.

[5] Loskiel, Hist. of Mission, pt. I, p. 67.

Iroquois territory, several of these in southwestern Ontario. Stone and flint implements suggesting use as hoes or spades have been found all over the alluvial lands on the Mississippi and its tributaries, as well as in the Iroquois country. The form most widely distributed is an of oval or elliptical outline, with rounded or pointed ends, some being notched for attachment to a handle, which may have been fastened on either parallel with the longer axis, or at an angle to it.[1]

Shell was evidently not favoured by the Iroquois as a material for hoes, though it was so employed by surrounding nations.[2] An Onondaga name for the latter implement is atcokdǫ῾sää'.

A wooden digging-stick or spade, ehe'di῾akta', is said to have been used as recently as sixty years ago. A model of this was constructed by an Onondaga informant.[3] A notch at one side afforded a place for the foot in digging. The implement was made of hardwood, such as white oak, ironwood, or hickory (Plate I, fig. a).

Special articles for carrying the seed-grain are practically non-existent at present, although the informant last mentioned remembered a flat-shaped planting-basket, with compartments for corn and the bean or squash seeds which are planted with it. This was carried in the hand, or was tied to the belt (Plate I, fig. c). The name applied was eyentwa῾tha' ga'a῾sää' (On.). The information was confirmed by other informants.[4] An ordinary small basket is often used at present.

A couple of types of elm bark planting basket are noted by A. C. Parker.[5] Bruyas records the term "assenonte," which signifies "a small sack which the women attach to the belt and in which is their grain for sowing."[6] Both the latter references suggest that splint basketry was less extensively used in the earlier days than at present.

---

[1] *Handbook of American Indians*, p. 555.

[2] Wintemberg, W. J., *The Use of Shell by the Ontario Indians*, Ont. Arch. Rep., 1907, p. 38.

[3] Peter John, Grand River reserve.

[4] Mrs. Maggie Hill (Ca.), and John Jamieson, jun., (Ca.), Grand River reserve.

[5] Parker, A. C., *N. Y. State Museum Bulletin 144*, plate 19.

[6] Bruyas, *Radices Verborum Iroquaeorum*.

EARLY DESCRIPTIONS OF CORN CULTURE.

The descriptions of corn cultivation by early writers are interesting for comparison. Hariot, in "A briefe and true report of the new found land of Virginia," remarks that "A few daies before they sowe or set, the men with wooden instruments, made almost in forme of mattockes or hoes with long handles; the women with short peckers or parers, because they use them sitting, of a foote long and about five inches in breadth: doe onely breake the upper part of the ground to rayse up the weedes, grasse, and old stubbles of corne stalkes with their roots." These were burned, no appreciation being shown of the ashes as a fertilizing material. Holes were made with a pecking instrument at about half a fathom or a yard apart and were arranged in rows. Four grains were put into each hole. In the spaces between the hills, according to this observer, were planted beans, pease, sunflowers, "macocqwer"or squash, and "melden."

A method of planting in beds or hills is described and illustrated by Lafitau, though unfortunately, like many others, he fails to specify to what tribe or nation he refers. He further informs us that "all that is necessary to them is a curved piece of wood, three fingers in width, and attached to a long handle, and which serves to cut down the weeds and to stir the soil a little." Gourds (citrouilles) and melons were planted in separate fields by these agriculturists. The seeds were first planted indoors between two pieces of bark, placed above their fireplaces, then transplanted.[1] A reference showing that the Iroquois were quite early acquainted with transplanting is found in Shea's French-Onondaga dictionary, where we find many other interesting agricultural terms.[2] Large stones were also sometimes placed among the young plants to prevent them from being killed by late frosts.[3]

Indian agriculture evidently had a most important bearing upon the struggle of the early colonists. In most cases starva-

---

[1] Lafitau, *Moeurs des Sauvages*, pt. II, pp. 76-78.

[2] Shea, J. G., *French-Onondaga Dictionary* (17th Century), see "Transplante."

[3] David Jack (Ca.).

tion would have ensued without the supplies either purchased or stolen from the Indians, and even at a later date, when the stability of the settlements was assured, the colonists were glad to adopt the cultivation of corn and other native products.

The "Armouchiquois" employed both fish and shell to enrich the soil.[1] The "Tsonnontouans," or Seneca, were said to "manure a great deal of ground for sowing their Indian corn in."[2] Carr makes the statement that the "Indian," generally, "understood and appreciated the benefits arising from the use of fertilizers."[3] This evidently did not apply to all the Iroquois. The Relation of 1638-39, for instance, remarks, regarding the Hurons, that "the land, as they do not cultivate it, produces for only ten or twelve years at most; and when the ten years have expired, they are obliged to move their village to another place."[4] A method of fertilization sometimes practised, according to Grand River Iroquois, was to make a corn-patch where a house had formerly stood.

At present, corn is occasionally planted in low-lying ground, without other cultivation or fertilization, the foot being used to scrape a hole for and to cover the grain.[5] Some of the older people consider that the corn is better when planted in the latter manner, although the custom may be the vestige of a taboo against soil disturbance, which was not unknown in this area.[6] An Onondaga informant stated that in his younger days the weeds were sometimes merely cleared away for a small space around the old cornstalk, which was then pulled, the corn being planted in the hollow left. This was called "ganä'gęse'tciy," or "scraping with the hoe and planting in the same place again."[7]

[1] Lescarbot, Paris, 1612, vol. II, p. 834.
[2] Hennepin, *A New Discovery*, R. G. Thwaites ed., p. 46.
[3] Carr, *Mounds of the Mississippi Valley*, Smithsonian Rep., 1891.
[4] *Jesuit Relations*, R. G. Thwaites ed., vol. XV, p. 153.
[5] John Echo and Peter John (On.); John Jamieson, jun. (Ca.).
[6] Boyle, David, *Arch. Rep. Ontario*, 1898, pp. 68, 69.
Mooney, Jas., *Ghost Dance Religion*, Annual Report, B. A. E., vol. XIV, pt. II.
[7] Peter John (On.).

CORN "MEDICINES."

When all is ready for planting, the corn is soaked in a decoction made of certain herbal ingredients. The moisture causes the corn to germinate slightly, though the utility of the added materials is not so evident. There is possibly some connexion with sympathetic magic, the other plants contributing their vitality, or otherwise assisting and protecting the corn. Regarding what appeared to be the oldest or, at any rate, the most important of these preparations, it was stated by a Cayuga informant[1] that it prevented the worms and birds from bothering. A sort of halo was also said to be sometimes seen around the plants.

A reference to corn medicines is found in the Code of Handsome Lake, the Iroquois prophet, as translated by A. C. Parker: "Now it is understood that Dio'he⁻kǫ (the corn, bean and squash spirits), have a secret medicine, o'saga'ndà and o'dɩ'sdani. So soak your seed corn in these two medicines before you plant your fields. The medicines grow on the flat lands near streams."[2]

The medicine referred to consists, according to Grand River informants, of the submerged rootstocks of *Phragmites communis*, a tall, reed-like grass growing in marshes; and *Hystrix patula*, or bottle-brush grass, also growing in low land. The former is called by Brant County Onondaga u'sa'gä'ą̈da'; the latter, gusdisda⁻nɩ'. According to Chief Gibson's directions,

---

[1] Chief David Jack, a Brant County Cayuga.

[2] Parker, A. C., *The Code of Handsome Lake*, N. Y. State Mus. Bulletin, 163, p. 54.

A story which may or may not account for the origin of "corn medicine" was given by John Echo (On.). This was to the effect that the Allegheny Iroquois once gathered up food and other material for a celebration of the before-planting or yundagǫ⁻'wi⁻'sa' ceremony. They also obtained a lot of whiskey, with which they put in a prolonged spree. This lasted so long that a month elapsed before they thought of planting their corn. In the fall when the frosts came the corn was still immature, so that they lost the whole crop. A voice—that of Hawäni'yu'—was heard. It said: "It is your own fault. You did wrong." He then went to one family which lived away by itself and had taken no part in the spree and told the members that the only way to escape permanent retribution for their foolishness was to use corn medicine. Skaniadai'iyu' afterward confirmed this.

the roots of a single bunch or cluster of each plant are to be taken, eight quarts of water added, and the whole boiled down to six. This is cooled, the seed corn added and left for an hour or so, after which it is drained, placed in a basket while still moist, and left until it sprouts a little. In olden times, according to David Jack, some one would bring a quantity of the root to the longhouse and each person who intended to plant anything would be given a piece. The directions of the latter informant were to take a whole plant of the bottle-brush grass[1] (Ca., gu'sdista‘) and about 4 inches of the rootstock of the phragmites (usa'’ge‘ɛnda'); these are crushed and added to about five quarts of warm water.

At Tonawanda, N.Y., wild rye (*Elymus canadensis*) was given instead of bottle-brush grass[2], one having possibly been confused with or substituted for the other. Seneca names for phragmites, given by Barber Black, were gasaⁿgeą̈da' and yenͻwɛⁿda‘gwa' oneͻ'.[3] Mrs. Peter Sundown, who comes from Alleghany, gave disdi'sdanɩ' for one ingredient.

Quite different materials from those named are used in some localities. Peter John, Onondaga, employed the leaves of the mandrake (*Podophyllum peltatum*). These were simply placed in the water, the flowers of the elder (*Sambucus canadensis*) being also sometimes added.

None of the medicines described are poisonous, although Kalm records the use of the wild hellebore (*Veratrum album*) by the Swedes and other colonists of the eastern states,[4] possibly in imitation of the Indians.

Sagard observed that the Hurons soaked their seed-grain in warm water, although no herbal ingredients are mentioned.[5]

---

[1] The same informant later showed a sample of nodding fescue grass, *Festuca nutans*, as the proper material, showing that some uncertainty exists regarding this ingredient, or that different grasses are used.

[2] Informant, Barber Black.

[3] The latter is simply a general name meaning "medicine for putting corn in." A Cayuga equivalent to this, given by David Jack, was enᾳhᾳwɛ' ‘da'kwa' onͻ'gwatra.

[4] Kalm, *Travels*, vol. II, pp. 91, 92.

[5] Sagard, *Grand Voyage*, Tross ed., pt. I, p. 93.

This seems to be the earliest record of any such custom. There is a possibility that a part of the process escaped his observation.

It is interesting for comparison to note that white people occasionally add oats to the water in which seed corn is germinated. Oats are also sometimes planted with cuttings of trees and shrubs.

PLANTING OF THE CORN.

After the corn medicine has been applied—to continue Chief Gibson's description—the family all turn out. The woman of the house stands in the middle of the field and offers up a brief invocation, using some such form of words as: "God, our Father, you see me and my children. We stand in the middle of the field where we are going to plant our food. We beg you to supply us with an abundant yield of corn." They then commence to plant, usually placing beans, squash seeds, or pumpkin seeds in every hill, or every few hills apart.

John Echo (On.), who lives in the same locality, described the man as the head of the family. The following was given as an example of the prayer offered: "Gaiạhia'de'si'dạ̈' sowäni'yu' o'näwa·'agwa·ade'sa' u'nä·ohe·dagǫ'wa ęyagowa'yę' ägionhe·gwı' unę'ha' unɛndi' wagwaiiwa'ne·gạ skänǫtǫseyagwatga'twa' unɛ'ndi' daskoạdạ̈'ạ̈·. This may be rendered freely as: "In the sky you live, Hawɛni'yu'. We are ready to place in the ground the corn upon which we live. We ask for assistance and that we may have a plentiful crop."

All the cultivation given formerly was to chop down the weeds, or to clear away the last year's cornstalks. The weeds which sprang up were either pulled up or trampled down.

A couple of beans, mentioned specially as cornstalk beans, were obtained from Mrs. Fannie Johnson of Tonawanda, whose grandmother had kept up their cultivation. One of these, called o'iä'gekaa', was buff with stripes of a very dark maroon, and of a short, flat shape. The other, a small, dark brown bean, was called oyę'gwä'ạ̈' (smoky-coloured).

The sunflower was also sometimes planted with the corn and beans, although it was perhaps more frequently cultivated in patches by itself. Kalm, in his visit to Lower Canada, noticed that the Hurons of Lorette "plant our common sunflower in their maize-fields, and mix the seeds of it into their sagamité, or maize-soup."[1]

A taboo in connexion with corn-planting was obtained from Mr. Seth Newhouse of Canienga. This was to the effect that a woman at the menstrual period should abstain from any part in planting operations.

The best time for corn-planting, according to Jacob Hess (Ca.), is when the first leaves appearing on the oak in spring are as big as a red squirrel's foot. This he believed to be an old Iroquois tradition.

It was remarked by John Echo (On.) that a reliable method was to plant the corn when the blossoms of the juneberry (*Amelanchier canadensis*), or gä'ä'duŋk appear. Peas, according to the same informant, are to be planted in the full of the moon. The latter idea is evidently a European borrowing.

Additional Terminology (Onondaga).

First hoeing, deyehe·'dawą'yιᵏk.
Second hoeing, deye·nondai·ets (puts its legs together).
I am through hoeing the corn, wagatędiˑsa'o'nɛ onɛ'ha'.
Planting time, tsa'niyeyɛntwahuŋk, or tsa'niyeyɛndo't'ha' (setting up a log)
Hill of corn, deye'nondai·ets.
Cornstalk, uhe·'ɛ'.
Corn pith, oha·'da'.
She is plucking the ripe corn, enǫ·gwayɛ·ntha' (all the crop taken).
She is plucking the green corn, enǫ·gwę·yu·'ne' (plucking a little green corn).
She cuts down the weeds, deyehe·dawą·yιk or agɛnu·ge·yɑks, or ehe·'daa·'s.
She is dropping or planting the corn, gonähǫ·'die's.
Milk or juice of corn, ogǫ·sä·'gei'.
She is husking corn, enoyu·ntha'.
A braid or string of corn, djusdę·'sä·'äda·.
He is making a string of corn, hastę·'sää·'niaha'.
They are making strings of corn, hadistę·'sää·'niaha'.
She is making a string of corn, ιstę·'sää·'niaha'.

---

[1] Kalm, *Travels*, vol. III, p. 164.

She is planting corn, eyɛ'ntwas.
The corn is sprouting, odiagɛ'ʾio'nɛ.
The ears are forming, ohwɛˑda'o'nɛ, or onǫgwɛ'yuwanɛ's (sing.).
Corn silk, ogeeˑda'.
The silk is forming, ogeeˑda'o'nɛ.
The tassel, ogwɛˑdaˑhää', or ogwɛˑdaˑhää'o'nɛ.
Pollen, awɛ'ha'.
The pollen is being shed, awɛ'ha' waⁿsɛ's.
The corn is in the milk, haˑsa'ʾ deyuisateˑk ą'ni'yut.
The green corn is ready for use (for boiling), ha'degaiyeˑi'o'nɛ ayenǫˑ-gwa'yoʾ.
The corn is getting ripe, deyonoyaneˑdao'nɛ (husk is getting yellow now).
Corn leaves, odjiǫwaˣso'wanɛ's.
Root (of corn), uheˑɛ' ukdeˑhä'.
Germ or heart of a grain of corn, aweyaⁿsa' onɛ'ha'.
Hull or skin, onɛ'ha', ogeeⁿgwa'.
Corn-cob, onǫˑgwąⁿya'.
The butt of a cob, u'ni'sda'.
The nose or end of a cob, o'niɥˑsa'.
The corn is hung over a pole, gastɛ'säˑniǫ'da' o'ąˑnaⁿgɩˑ.

THANKSGIVING AFTER PLANTING.

After planting, the people meet again to thank the Great Mother and also to give thanks "direct to God"—to use Chief Gibson's phraseology—that they have got through with this part of their labours. The speaker at this ceremony asks the Thunder Man to protect the plants and to bring the rain or moisture to wet the ground and to make them grow. The Onondaga name given for the Thunder Man is Etiso'da' Hadiwɛnoda'die's, the Grandfather of all. A Seneca equivalent is Hi'nǫ'.

The duty of the Thunder Men individually and collectively is to carry water to dampen and wash the earth and to renew the water in the streams, creeks, and lakes. They must, therefore, be thanked, as well as the Sun, Moon, and other deities, and asked to protect and prosper the crops.

CULTIVATION CEREMONIALS.

When the corn is up there is another meeting and a dance, also when the first cultivating and hoeing are finished. One of the chief speakers addresses the people, giving thanks and "congratulating" them on having done their duty in assisting our Great Mother. He next addresses God, thanking him and asking him to give an abundant yield. Two singers are then appointed and the Great Feather Dance performed. The first hoeing is called in Onondaga deyehe'dawą'yιk or deyehe'dawąye'haŋk, the latter name denoting a large number of people working.

The second cultivation takes place, according to the informant,[1] when the corn is about 2 feet high, and a meeting is again held. This cultivation is called deye'nǫdai'i'ga', or hilling up. At each of these meetings corn soup is made and distributed equally among those present.

Invocations or prayers to the Thunder Men may be offered at any or all of the meetings, as may seem desirable. If the weather is too hot or dry, special gatherings may be called for such invocations and are considered highly effective and beneficial.[2]

RAIN-MAKING.

Ceremonies for producing or controlling rain have been practised by most North American tribes and are frequently described by the earlier travellers and others. These seem, among the Iroquois, to have been mostly shamanistic, or one-man performances, which were later incorporated as regular religious functions or ceremonials.

Le Jeune, in the Relation of 1636, describes the rain-making performances of a Huron medicine-man: "All were crying for help, and imploring, according to their custom, the help of the sorcerers, or Arendiowane. . . . These deceivers played all the tricks that dreams and their own empty heads could suggest to them in order to bring rain, but in vain. . . . There was one of these sorcerers named Tehorenhaegnon, more famous than the others, who promised marvels, provided the whole country made him a present of the value of ten hatchets, not to speak of a multitude of feasts; but these efforts were in vain—dreaming, feasting, dancing, were all to no purpose." This

---

[1] Chief Gibson.

[2] Cf. Caswell, H. S., *Our Life Among the Iroquois*, p. 217.

3

"soothsayer" gave as a reason for his non-success, "that the thunder, which they pretend is a bird, was afraid of the cross that was in front of the Frenchman's house."[1]

The Petuns, or Tobacco Nation, another cognate tribe, possessed performers of a similar type: "Onditachiae is renowned . . . from having in hand the rains, the winds, and the thunder. This thunder is, by his account, a man like a turkey-cock; the sky is his palace, and he retires there when it is serene; he comes down to earth to get his supply of adders and serpents, and of all they call Oki, when the thunder is rumbling; the lightnings occur in proportion as he extends or folds his wings. If the uproar is a little louder, it is his little ones who accompany him, and help him to make a noise as best they can."

Dryness, according to this sorcerer, came from caterpillars, over which he had no control.

Le Jeune further states, with regard to the Thunder, that "the Hurons believed it to be a very large bird. They were led to this belief by a hollow sound made by a kind of swallow (evidently the night-hawk, *Chordeiles virginianus*) which appears here in the summer . . . they fly about in the evening, repeatedly making a dull noise. The Hurons say they make this noise from behind,[2] as does also the bird which they think is the thunder." This information was obtained from the Montagnais, who added that "it ate snakes and sometimes trees."[3]

Among the Iroquois proper and a number of the eastern Algonkin tribes, the Thunder-bird idea is replaced by that of the Thunder Men, usually four in number, who control the rain and thunder. In a mythological sketch received from Chief Gibson, the Thunder Men were represented as hurling thunderbolts at a huge serpent which they are believed to have in charge. A common Oneida term for thunder is ga'sagaiyaont, "the Thun-

---

[1] *Jesuit Relations*, R. G. Thwaites ed., vol. X, pp. 35, 37.

Cf. also pp. 193, 195.

Cf. Loskiel, *Hist. of Mission*, pt. I, p. 46.

[2] The name for this bird at present in use among the Onondaga refers to this supposed characteristic.

[3] *Jesuit Relations*, R. G. Thwaites ed., vol. VI, p. 225.

derer, our Grandfather."[1] Low or distant thunder is caused
by a human being who was captured by the Thunder Men and
made to replace one of their number who was killed by a giant
blood-sucker or leech.[2]

The special ceremonial at present held for invoking rain
is described by Chief Gibson as follows: A meeting is called.
The chiefs appoint one man to be speaker, while the younger
members or warriors (hodisgạ̈ạ̈giˠdaꞌ) are often stripped to the
waist, or clad only in a breech-cloth. When the warriors are
ready, the old people make a fire near the west end of the longhouse. The speaker tells the people to go towards the fire.
All have some Indian tobacco, which they have been requested
by the speaker to bring. This is deposited in a basket held
by one of the older chiefs. An old woman is now selected to
get water from the creek. The braves are called to stand surrounding the fire, also the woman who has been appointed to
get the water, while the speaker prepares to burn the tobacco.[3]
These are the only ones who take an active part in the ceremony.

Then the speaker (a chief) calls "ku ku ku" in a high key.
He then speaks loudly and says: "You have heard the voice
from the people on earth direct to you, Thunder Man. The
people ask you to supply us rain to wet the earth and renew
the streams, creeks, and lakes." He next picks up the tobacco,
throws it into the fire, and says: "This is the tobacco, the
people's word for speaking direct to you. We are very anxious
to have rain, as it is dry weather on earth and it is very hard

---

[1] Mrs. David Williams, Oneidatown, Ontario.

[2] John Jamieson, jun. and others. The writer has more extended information in MSS.

[3] Mrs. E. A. Smith, in *Myths of the Iroquois*, says: "In a dry season, the
horizon being filled with distant thunder heads, it was customary to burn
what is called by the Indians real tobacco as an offering to bring rain.

On occasions of this nature the people were notified by swift-footed heralds
that the children, or sons, of Thunder were in the horizon, and that tobacco
must be burned in order to get some rain." 2nd Ann. Rep., B.A.E., 1880-81,
p. 72.

Cf. Heckewelder, Phila., 1819, p. 229.

Williams, Roger, *Key*, pt. I, p. 70, notes the existence of "meetings"
to pray for rain among the Narraganset and Eastern Indians.

on us that there is to be a failure of whatever grows on earth.
So we ask you to give us rain." Then, taking up the tobacco
again, he says: "Here is the tobacco, the people's word to you."
The braves now dance the wasaˀsⵝ.[1] The speaker says: "When
they get through the dance, we shall expect you to get rain for
us." The tobacco throwing is repeated twice more with a
similar invocation in each case.

When the speaker gets through, the people go into the
longhouse, with the exception of the warriors and the woman
with the water. As soon as the people have all got inside, the
warriors give three cheers. Two men who have been appointed
as singers then take, one a drum, the other a rattle, and begin
singing as soon as the cheers are given. Then the woman with
the pail scatters water towards the warriors at the fire, using
her hands for the purpose. The warriors now begin to dance,
moving slowly towards the longhouse. The dancers sometimes
whoop and shout very loudly, "like thunder," until they get
into the longhouse. The woman follows, sousing them with
water as they go. They continue dancing inside for a time.
A number of the old men and women then make speeches giving
thanks. Anyone wishing to speak has a stick and strikes on
the wall or floor; then the singers and dancers stop. This is
called çhanegwaˀeiʹgwaʹ (whoever wishes to speak), the expression called out by the person desiring to take his turn at speech-
making.

One of the chiefs generally speaks first, and may use some
such form as: "It is generally beneficial throughout the world
to have rain. I thank you, warriors, for your performance.
We give thanks to the Thunder. You'll supply us with water
to dampen the earth and plants. We thank you, our Father
which art in heaven." He then hands a small bundle of Indian
tobacco to the leader of the dance and says: "This is my word
for speaking direct to you, etc." The performers then dance
and cheer again. The striking with the stick is continued by
others who desire to speak. The women generally bring cakes

---

[1] It was stated that this is called a war-dance now, but that it is not
really such. It is referred to by A. C. Parker in *The Code of Handsome Lake*,
N.Y. State Mus. Bulletin, 163, p. 104, as the "Thunder Dance."

of some kind and when they give them they say, "This is my word." Near the close of this part of the proceedings the speaker congratulates them and says: "We hope the Thunder will approve of what we ask."

Corn soup is a necessity and an announcement is now made that this will be distributed equally among the people.

Sometimes, before they are through, the thunder may be heard, or often the next day it will rain. A name given for this ceremony was hadistai῾ndie῾ta'.[1] It was remarked by another informant that two women were chosen for the water-throwing performance, one for the deer side, the other for the mud-turtle.[2]

A method for rain-making given by Barber Black, of Tonawanda, was to take a little piece of the bark of a walnut tree where it has been struck by lightning. When the weather is too dry, place this in a cup of water, and leave for a couple of minutes. It will then rain in two days.

According to a couple of Grand River informants,[3] pointing at a storm which is going around will cause it to come back. This was contradicted by Peter John (On.) of the same locality, who said the belief was that pointing at the storm would make it go away.

It was stated by John Jamieson, jun., that toads should not be killed, but, that if one were killed and turned over on its back, rain would be produced.

A method of turning a thunderstorm aside was given by Mrs. David Williams, Oneidatown, Ontario. She had seen her father undertake this at one time by sticking the handle of an axe in the ground with the sharp edge pointing towards the approaching cloud[4].

---

[1] For reference to thunder ceremony, see Morgan, *League of the Iroquois*, vol. I, p. 188.

[2] The phratric division is often referred to by naming one of the clans on each side.

[3] John Jamieson, jun., and Chief J. H. Gibson.

[4] Sagard was asked by some Hurons to "kill the thunder," which they believed to be a bird. *Voyage*, vol. I, p. 175.
Cf. also Bartram, *Observations*, p. 68.

The same method was referred to by informants at other places. An interesting parallel with this idea is to be found in the following from Le Jeune's Relation of 1636: "Father Buteux asked a savage (Montagnais) why they fixed their javelins' point upward. He replied that, as the thunder had intelligence, it would, upon seeing these naked javelins, turn aside, and would be very careful not to come near their cabins."[1]

A storm on the Great Lake of the Hurons was explained as follows to Lalement: "After having in vain exhausted both their skill and their strength in resisting the tempest, they began to despair; they invoked a certain Demon named Iannaoa, who, they say, once cast himself into this lake in his despair, and causes all these storms when he wishes to revenge himself upon men; and he calms them after men have paid him some homage. In his honour, they throw tobacco into the water, which in these countries is a kind of sacrifice."[2]

A description of rain-making obtained by Dr. Boyle from William Bill, a Brant County Iroquois, contains the following method of stopping rain: "If I want to stop rain, just put some ashes and coal and some tobacco in a little tin dish, and look toward the west, and just watch it."[3]

Previous to the rain-making ceremony, according to John Jamieson, jun., a number of active young men used to be sent out to hunt for the splinters from trees which had been struck by lightning. The fire for the ceremony was kindled near sundown from this material, and was usually very small or just large enough to consume the ceremonial tobacco.

As the tobacco was placed on the fire, an invocation or prayer was offered asking for rain to make the corn, potatoes, and other products grow. The woman with the water next picked up the charred wood from the fire and put it into the pail which she held, after which more tobacco was offered and power asked for the water to wet the corn and other crops.

---

[1] *Jesuit Relations*, R. G. Thwaites ed., vol. X, p. 25.

For a Cherokee method of "frightening a storm" see *Bur. of Eth. Rep., 1885-86*, pp. 387-388.

[2] *Jesuit Relations*, R. G. Thwaites ed., vol. XXVI, pp. 309,311.

[3] Boyle, Dr. David, *Arch. Rep., Ontario, 1902*, p. 184.

Good luck was asked for everybody. The woman then threw the burnt wood out of the pail, the water contained in it being afterward used to sprinkle the dancers.

OTHER PLANTING TIME CUSTOMS AND BELIEFS.

Incantations or divination with a view to finding out what sort of crop may be expected seem to have been practised at times. A lightning-bug (On., djistäno'gą'), or a cicada (On., ganahaiita⁓gwa', "corn-ripener"), for instance, flying inside the house after corn or other seeds are planted, is the sign of a bountiful harvest.[1] The desired information may be gathered, as already noted, from the success or otherwise of the women in the peach-stone game at the spring meeting of the ǫtǫwi⁓zas, though it is probable that shamanistic performances were frequently resorted to formerly. We have, in fact, a suggestion of this in the Relation of 1642-43, in which we are informed that among the Hurons "the famous Magician in the Country was consulted to learn what success might be expected from the corn that had been planted." The exact method of procedure is not given, although the people were required to go every day to their fields, make an offering of tobacco and call upon the "Demon" or deity, which they worshipped.[2]

The services of fortune-tellers are still in requisition, as in many white communities, for such purposes as dream-interpretation, the finding of lost articles, the solution of love affairs, and the prognostication of success or non-success in agricultural and other undertakings.

WEATHER-LORE.[3]

According to Peter John (On.), a sure sign of rain is the series of small explosions or puffs heard during the combustion of hardwood fuel; the cackling or calling, while flying, of the great crested or pileated woodpecker, gwę⁓gwę; the leaping and falling backward of a sturgeon in the water.

---

[1] Peter John, John Echo, and others.
[2] *Jesuit Relations*, R. G. Thwaites ed., vol. XXIII, p. 35.
[3] A small collection of Iroquois omens is given by Hewitt in the *Amer. Anthrop.*, 1890.

Lots of husk on an ear of corn means a cold winter, while little husk indicates a mild winter.

Ice making a loud report is the sign of a thaw; also mice coming out and running about on the snow, as indicated by their tracks. The latter was considered a particularly reliable sign by the informant.

It was stated by Mrs. David Williams (Oneida) that cold weather may be produced by burning the boughs of the hemlock, onaꞥTA. Dr. Boyle notes that the performance of the "Skeleton Dance" in the spring is thought to be productive of frost.[1]

The following were given by Chief David Key, Seneca—the names are in Onondaga:

When a man is smoking and the smoke blows in a streak to one side, it will rain in twenty-four hours. The tobacco used must be oyę'gwaǫ'wι', or Iroquois native tobacco (*Nicotiana rustica*).

Cirrus clouds mean rain in a short time.

A robin (djisgaꞥga') sitting on the very top of a tree and singing is a sign of rain; also flying-squirrels sticking their heads out of their nests in hollow trees and emitting a call.

When it rains during a new moon it will be soft all month, also if a warm west wind comes up at a similar period.

A new moon lying horizontally means lots of rain; standing up pretty straight it means plenty of snow.

Whirlwinds (uwä'da'se') are a sign of dry weather, also cumulus clouds. The latter also foretell high winds. John Jamieson, jun., furnished the additional item regarding whirlwinds, that a short piece of hair would be found in the centre of the spot where a whirlwind has been seen. If this be picked up it will cause larger ones to come and destroy your buildings.

Muskrat houses built large and thick indicate cold weather and high water. You will also see the tracks of the animals in the snow where they have got away to safety.

Northern lights (duwääniꞥhwɑs, "raining away out") indicate that the rain or snow is all over and that the weather

---

[1] Boyle, David, *Arch. Rep. Ontario, 1898*, p. 130.

will be dry or cold. The name watowe'tht' (On.) given by John Echo, was translated as "going to have cold weather."

An eclipse (wadä⁓gwa'duŋk, "hid the moon or sun") means a change in the weather.

Signs furnished by John Echo were:

The hooting of a horned owl (On., degą'skt') is a sign of rain or snow.

To hear chopping or shouting plainly at a greater distance than usual is a sign of rain in a very few days.

When the streak of fat on the kidney of an animal like a deer or bear is thick all along it will be cold weather. When thick at either end and thin at the other it will be cold or warm at corresponding parts of the season.

John Jamieson, jun., stated that:

Sun-dogs (On., deyäouʋ'gwę, "throws the sunshine") are a sign of warm weather.

Hens sitting on the top of a fence or gate in the daytime is a sign of rain, also corn leaves curling up with the heat.

A meteor moving somewhat horizontally and in a northerly direction, if seen in the autumn or winter, is a sign of warm weather. One moving in an opposite direction is said to be going after cold weather.

An item by Chief David Jack was to the effect that when the Milky Way (Ca., uha'de' udji⁓sǫda', "pathway, starry") stands north and south, warm weather is indicated. Lying east and west means cold weather.

Others by the same informant were:

The Pigeon Dance should not be put on during the Maple Sugar Festival, or it will cause high winds, the movement of the air by the pigeons' wings being considered significant (sympathetic magic).

Pointing at a storm will bring bad luck. If it has passed it will come back. Pointing at a rainbow is also unlucky, as it will make you crooked. The Cayuga word for rainbow is diyu'ⁿhyud.

Jacob Hess (Ca.) stated that there is thought to be a creature or being called gatsgowęde'ⁿta', which consists of a pointed portion, with a long tail of hair trailing behind. This was seen at one time stuck into a tree. The tail was waving and the trees were uprooted all around it. This creature is considered to be the cause of high winds, and cyclones.

Many of the foregoing are distinctly Indian, although some European borrowing is also evident.

David Key (On.), an old hunter, stated that:

Owls calling near at hand in the bush means more snow or a change in the weather. Lots of wood should be gathered (as the conditions may not be favourable for gathering it later).

A flying-squirrel's calling near a man's hunting-shanty means snow before daylight.

If a skunk's or a coon's feet are well furred there will be a cold winter.

Thunder in the early spring, according to S. Anderson (Mo.), is a sign of an early thaw and spring weather.

An eclipse (Ca., wawadä''gwa''dǫ' aga'gwa''dǫ'), according to Thomas Smoke, when seen towards the south is indicative of early cold weather in the autumn. Seen towards the east it denotes mild weather all winter.

John Jamieson, sen. (On.) gave the following list:

Gulls' calling along a lake or river means rain.

A robin sitting on top of a tree and calling is a sign of rain. It is believed that he can see it coming and that he faces in the direction from which it will come.

If a deer's melt is equally thick all along there will be a steady, cold winter. If smaller at one end and larger at the other, it will be warmer and colder at corresponding parts of the season.

Snow-fleas indicate soft weather. The fleas are called odji'nǫ'wa' or swine''di' dji'nǫ'wa' (On., soft weather fleas).

A screech-owl (gwai'iwę) calling in the winter indicates that the weather will be milder.

A horse's or cow's shaking the body means snow or rain.

IROQUOIS CALENDARS.

Among the Iroquois there seems to have been a general division of the year into periods corresponding more or less closely with our spring, summer, autumn, and winter, besides that into moons or months. Loskiel remarks of the Delawares and the Iroquois that they "divide the year into winter, spring, summer and autumn, and each quarter into months, but their calculations are very imperfect, nor can they agree when to begin the new year. Most of them begin with the spring, some with any other quarter, and many, who are acquainted with the Europeans, begin with our New Year's day." His interpretations of the names given to the months, however, differ from those which follow.[1]

Among some eastern woodland tribes there was a division into ten moons or months. One of the Relations remarks that "the greater part of the savages admit only ten moons." This evidently referred more particularly to the Algonkins. The Iroquois apparently agree upon twelve divisions,[2] the influence of environment and occupation being shown by the names, which refer to the weather or the natural products growing or maturing at the seasons indicated.

The following names of the seasons were furnished by Jacob Hess (Ca.), Chief David Key (Seneca speaking Onondaga), and Paul Jacobs (Mo. of Caughnawaga):

Spring:
> gagwi'di or gägwi'di (Ca.)[3]
> gagwi'dini' (Ca., "towards spring")
> gogwide'anı' (Mo.)
> diyųgwagähọ'dı' (On.)
> yęrą'ke·'ⁿde (Wyandot, "it, turn over, is coming.")
> General meaning: It is time to plant or sow.[4]

Summer:
> agǫha'gı' (Mo.)
> a·wàyę·'rą (Wyandot) } "it turns over, is coming"
> ganä'na'gı' (On.)
> wàyęnte·''ye (Wyandot) } "it red has come"

---

[1] Loskiel, *Hist. of Mission*, p. 29.

[2] *Jesuit Relations*, R. G. Thwaites ed., vol. VI, p. 223.

[3] A similar term, keng8ite (kengwite) is given in the French-Onondaga dictionary of the 17th century, edited by Shea.

[4] Analyses of the terms were furnished by Mr. C. M. Barbeau.

Autumn:

agą'tr'dą (Ca.) ⎫
agątr'dąu'na (Ca.) ⎬ "self, leaves fall"

ganenage˄ni' (Ca.)[1] ⎫
gɑna'ge'anı' (Mo.) ⎪
yànᵉⁿda·'ᵃyę'de (Wyandot) ⎬ "the red colours have come'
ganąna˄ge'hagwadı' (On.) ⎭

Winter:

gu'sä'ä'gı' (On.)
ogosera'gı' (Mo.)
go'sri'niuna (Ca.)
yu'cre·'de (Wyandot)

General meaning: The cold has arrived.

First-hand versions of the names of the Iroquois months were obtained from the late Chief Gibson, Seneca speaking Onondaga, and from Chief David Skye, Onondaga. These two are substantially in agreement, although the Seneca and Onondaga differ as to the beginning of the Indian new year and the date of the ceremonies connected therewith. The names recorded are compared with those obtained by J. N. B. Hewitt from the late Chief John Buck (On.), those given in the French Onondaga dictionary (edited by Shea), and with those of a missionary calendar in the possession of Mr. Stacey, a Caughnawaga Iroquois.

1. disgu·'na', principal mid-winter month; begins first new moon after January 1 (Chief John Gibson, Seneca, Brant County reserve).

  dis-go'-na, days great or longer (Hewitt, J. N. B.).

  anisgo'wa, March (from calendar in possession of Stacey, Mohawk, Caughnawaga).

  tichkona, very windy month (Shea's ed. of a French-Onondaga dictionary of the 17th century).

  Meaning:[2] the sun is large again.

---

[1] Shea gives kanenaque.

[2] From analyses furnished by Mr. C. M. Barbeau, division of anthropology Geological Survey, Canada.

2. ganä'du'ha', month following disgu'na'; said by informant to mean leaves falling into the water from such trees as the oak and beach, to which they have clung during the winter. (Chief Gibson): February.

   ka-näq-to-ha, somewhat immersing the leaves (Hewitt).

   onera'do'ga, April (Stacey's calendar).

   ganerattoha, April (Shea).

   Meaning: leaves (fall) down into the water.

3. ganä'du'gu''na, great falling (of) leaves under the water now (Chief Gibson): March.

   ka-naq-to-go'-na, thoroughly immersing the leaves (Hewitt).

   onera'dogo'wa, May (Stacey's calendar).

   ganerattogona, May (Shea).

   Meaning: the leaves are quite or much immersed.

4. he'sɑtɑ', bushes, shrubs, and plants begin to grow again (Chief Gibson): April.

   heq-sat-à, slight freezing (Hewitt).

   ichakka, June (Shea).

   Meaning: it (the plants or vegetation) stands up again.

5. u'hiaïgu''na', or hiaïha, berries begin to ripen (Chief Gibson); another informant, Peter John (On.), gave uhiaïï'ha.

   hiaiigu''na', May (Chief Skye).

   hya-i-hà', fruits begin to ripen (Hewitt).

   ohiari'ha, June (Stacey's calendar).

   hiarigôna, July (Shea).

   Meaning: fruits are getting ripe, or are quite ripe.

6. sɪsge'ha', plants growing (Chief Gibson): June.

   sɪs-ke-hà (Hewitt).

   sesge'a', August (Stacey's calendar).

   Chereske'ha,[1] August (Shea).

7. sɪsgegu''na', almost everything growing up and bearing something (Chief Gibson): July.

   sis-ke-go''na (Hewitt).

   sesgego'wa, September (Stacey's calendar).

   chereske'gona, September (Shea).

---

[1] The accent following *e*, in names from the French-Onondaga calendar, is the French *e* acute.

Meaning: same as preceding plus suffix meaning greatly or abundantly.

8. gädę"a', food beginning to form (Chief Gibson): August.
kę-tę'-a' (Hewitt).
gantą'ha, October (Stacey).
kentenha, October (Shea).
Meaning: the field falls or is coming down, the harvest is gathered.

9. gädę'a'gu·'na', season when everything is bearing food (Chief Gibson): September.
kę-tę'-go'-nà, (Hewitt).
gątągo'wa, November (Stacey).
kentengôna, November (Shea).
Meaning: it field falls down much, the field is quite harvested.

10. djutu'weha', beginning of cold weather (Chief Gibson): October.
tco-tho-we-ha, again it is somewhat cold (Hewitt).
djodo'ra', December (Stacey).
dziotore'ha, December (Shea).
General meaning: again it is cold coming; i.e. the cold is coming again.

11. djutuwęgu·'na', beginning of cold weather (Chief Gibson): November.
tco-tho-we-go'-nà, again it is greatly cold (Hewitt).
djodor'go'wa, January (Stacey).
dziotoragona, Moon of Great cold (Shea).
Meaning: again it is cold greatly.

12. disa', (Chief Gibson) disɑ', (Chief Skye) }December.
dɩs-à', short days (Hewitt).
ani'ska, February (Stacey).
tichha, windy (?) moon (Shea).
Probable meaning: the sun is returning.

PROTECTION OF CROPS.

Among the most persistent corn-thieves were the crow, ga" ga' (On.), and the blackbird, djukgii'sda'gagowa'nε (On.).

These were either frightened away or captured by means of a noose or snare attached to a bent-over sapling, grains of corn being scattered about as a bait.

Later on there were the raccoon, djo'a'gɑk (On.); and the woodchuck, una''gent, attacking the fields along the borders of woods and clearings; or the muskrat, hanu'’gie‘, who visits the corn-patches lying along rivers and creeks. Many contrivances were designed for the capture of these, all based upon an intimate knowledge of wood-craft. The raccoon's habit of reaching with his forefeet suggested a small opening with some attractive bait at the farther end, a number of closely converging points preventing withdrawal. Deadfalls, with or without bait, were also used effectively.[1]

When the corn was ripe and suspended outside upon poles to dry, it was often stolen by jays and crows. These were caught by means of a slab of bark of suitable length and width, with holes cut along the middle to admit the head. Loops or nooses of basswood inner bark were arranged around these openings and the contrivance was placed on top of the racks of corn. The rest of the grain was covered and the birds, in reaching for it through the holes in the bark, became entangled in the nooses.[2]

A dead crow or jay, di'’di (On.), suspended by the legs near a corn-crib or in a cornfield, furnished an example to evil-doers. A custom still followed is to take a young crow and hang it up by the legs alive.

A device employed for frightening birds was a cylindrical whistle, suspended from a pole. This was operated upon by the wind and is said to have been suggested by an old man who discovered that the wind made a noise upon his flute when he hung it outside. The whistles were formerly made of wooden cylinders, closed at one end. Bottles are often used for the purpose now. An Onondaga name for the whistle is watą̈'doya'‘a' (things planted, to scare anything from).[3]

---

[1] John Jamieson, jun. (Ca.). Various types of Iroquois traps will be described in detail in a later paper of this series.

[2] Chief Gibson and others.

[3] John Jamieson, jun. (Ca.).

END OF SEASON CEREMONY.

At the end of the season there is another meeting or session of the Qtǫwi˄zɑs, at which the procedure is much the same as previously outlined, except that the peach-stone game is not played. This is the season when the corn is ready to store away and thanks must again be given for food. This ceremony is called ą̊yǫtä'gwaie˄ga' (gathering corn bread). Nearly every family prepares for this by baking a batch of old-fashioned corn bread. This is brought to the longhouse. A speaker is again appointed and addresses the people, congratulating them on the success of their crop or harvest. Thanks are also given to the Great Spirit that the people have been well supplied. Two men are then appointed to perform the Great Feather Dance. After this there is another dance for females only, called owɛsga′nii' (to thank the Great Mother and Three Sisters). This ends what Chief Gibson referred to as "the first part of the programme."

The second part is the ga'datshe˄'da', sometimes rendered as the "Trotting Dance." All take part in this, which is also a giving of thanks to the Great Mother and Three Sisters.

The third part is participated in by women only. It is also called owɛsga′nii', and is the second dance in which the women alone take part, being thus privileged, as Chief Gibson remarked, on account of the nature of the proceedings.

The fourth part is called deyǫdadɛnę'tcąus (joining their hands, or union).[1] All join hands in this and dance. The women have the "privilege" of joining hands with the men. This is said to typify the mixing or joining of the seeds in the hills of corn. On the other hand, the women may remain together. Children also take part in this dance. Other dances may also be performed.

When through with this portion of the proceedings, the people are addressed by the speaker, who thanks them and the Creator that they have got through with their duty. The speaker then reminds them of the Midwinter Festival, which comes in the

---

[1] This is sometimes translated as the Snake Dance.

month of Disgu·'na', on the fifth day of the new moon. He also asks those who are going into the forest to hunt, or on any similar expedition, to remember to return by this date.

HARVESTING AND STORAGE.

The most ancient method of harvesting consisted merely in gathering the ripened ears from the standing corn, the stalks being allowed to remain as already noted, until the next season's operations necessitated their removal. The ears were plucked, usually with the right hand, and thrown backward over the same shoulder into the gathering basket, e·nähanę'gwi·ta' (On.) or egehąąda·'kwa', which was suspended from the back by a burden strap (Plate XXII, fig. e). The basket was emptied by bringing it forward over the head and dropping it bottom upward upon the pile.[1] The gathering basket is sometimes emptied into a still larger basket which is provided with handles on opposite sides so that it can be carried by two persons.

The same informant states that a hut or house of corn-stalks was formerly constructed in the field as a shelter for the huskers. This was made like the old-style bark house (Plate IV).

A very common method at present is to tie the stalks, with the ears attached, into large bundles, sometimes with strings of hickory bark. These are allowed to stand in the field until the corn dries slightly, after which the ears are plucked and husked.

The old style of husking was to sit upon the ground with the legs straight, or with one knee slightly elevated. Four husks were usually left upon each ear for braiding, the rest were removed and carefully laid aside for use in mat-making, etc. Those employed in braiding knelt on one knee (Plate V). An ear with the husks pulled back for this purpose is called in Onondaga ganu'yu'nda' or waiinọ'gwę'yo'gaa', and with the husks entirely removed, wa'inuwi'iyɑk or udnoya·'gı'. The latter name is also applied to stunted ears or nubbins, which are not made into strings, but are merely thrown upon the floor to dry.[2]

---

[1] Peter John (On.) and others.

[2] Peter John.

A string of corn is called ustęⁿsää' (On.), and is usually five spans (hwiks niyuwę''gage') in length.

The husks are torn apart by means of a husking pin of hickory or other hardwood, though bone is sometimes used (Plate VI, figs. a and b). A name used for this implement is enuiya'kta' ga'wɑ'sta' (On.). It is possible that many of the stout awl-like bone implements, which are found on ancient village sites, were used for this purpose. The bones of the bear seem to have been a popular material, and the young people sometimes practised a species of divination by bending these articles slightly, an easily broken pin indicating a short life. Chief Gibson had frequently seen husking-pins made from the ribs of animals, such as the deer. The husking-pins employed at present have a groove around the middle, affording attachment to a leather loop, which is slipped over the middle finger. The pin is grasped in the palm, then stuck, with a vigorous sweep, into the leafy covering, the thumb closed down tightly and the husks torn back in preparation for braiding.

The husking bee, hadinowi'yake' (removing all the husks), gave rise to many social gatherings from house to house, at which corn soup was distributed liberally and where the proceedings were often enlivened with dancing or story-telling. A game formerly played on such occasions consisted in piling up short pieces of cornstalk into a house-like structure and endeavouring to flip these away one at a time without knocking down the others.[1]

An interesting description is given by Sagard of Huron harvesting: "The grain ripens in four months, and in certain places in three; afterwards they pluck it, tie it by the husks or leaves, which are pulled back, in this manner forming bundles or strings, which they suspend the length of the cabins, from top to bottom, on poles which they place in the form of racks, descending to the outer edge of the sleeping platforms, and all so neatly done that they seem to be tapestries or curtains stretched along the cabins, and the grain being thoroughly dried and ready for storing away, the women and girls shell it, clean it, and place it in their great vats (cuves) or casks (tonnes) made

---

[1] David Jack, Ca.

for this purpose and placed in their porches or in some corner of the cabin."[1]

The corn crib, ga'ⁿhe·'da'[2] is a favourite storage device among the Iroquois, although the strings of corn are sometimes suspended in the garret[3] or other parts of the house. Poles are placed across, about 2½ feet apart, and the strings thrown over these. The cribs at present are usually constructed of boards, with shingled roofs (Plates VII, VIII). In many cases a tin pan is inverted over each of the corner posts upon which the building is placed, to prevent the mice and squirrels from ascending. A few are made of poles, usually with a simple "lean-to" roof (Plate IX). The cobs are either thrown loosely into these, or the braids thrown over poles which are arranged inside.

A method of divination, according to John Jamieson, jun., was formerly practised as follows: a cob of corn was placed in the edge of the fire by a warrior who was about to go to war. After an hour or so he would return. If the cob, in the meantime, had been entirely consumed, it signified that he would be killed in battle.

A quite different style of crib or storage receptacle from those described was stated by Chief Gibson to have been used within his recollection. This was round and was sometimes made higher than the ordinary crib. A suggestion of the shape is contained in the name, ga'na'gu'uda', which signifies "barrel set." It was made by taking small posts, up to 6 inches in diameter, for the wall. A hole was next dug about 1½ feet deep and as large around as required. The posts were set closely around the circumference of the hole, the dirt thrown in up to the level of the ground and packed down solidly. This barrel-shaped receptacle was filled with the corn in the cob and poles were laid straight across the top. Over these were placed flat pieces of elm bark, which were removed from the tree in the spring and seasoned during the summer. Another pole was

---

[1] Sagard, *Voyage*, vol. I, pp. 93, 94.

[2] Peter John, Onondaga, gives enahaiyɛnda·'kwa' as a better name.

[3] Storage in garrets is mentioned by both Cartier and Champlain.

placed on top of the bark and the ends tied down with strips of basswood inner bark.

Le Jeune mentions the "granaries or chests of corn" in use among the Hurons.[1] These were evidently large box or barrel-like vessels which were placed inside the cabins. Champlain remarks, with regard to the same nation, that "at the end of these cabins is a space where they keep their corn, which they place in large casks, made of the bark of trees."[2] Both elm and birchbark were used for such utensils, as well as for many other household purposes. Remains of birchbark boxes or storage receptacles have been found on Huron and other village sites.[3]

The size of some of these casks or bins may be gathered from an item in the Relations, which mentions the possession by a Huron of two bins which held at least one hundred to one hundred and twenty bushels. Lafitau, in speaking of the interior household arrangements of the Iroquois and the construction of sleeping platforms, remarks that "the barks which enclose the platforms at the top and which form the canopy of the bed, take the place of a wardrobe or pantry, where they place, in view of everybody, their dishes and utensils. Between the platforms are placed great boxes (caisses) of bark, in the form of casks (tonnes) and five or six feet high, where they place their corn when it is shelled."[4]

The construction of storage pits was evidently quite common among the Iroquois, for caches while travelling, to guard against the capture of their supplies by enemies, and for the preservation of such garden products as squashes, pumpkins, etc. Lafitau, in describing this custom, states that "the Indian women make . . . . . . underground storage places in their fields, in which to place their squashes (citrouilles) and other fruits, which can only in this way be protected from the severity

---

[1] *Jesuit Relations*, R. G. Thwaites ed., vol. XVII, p. 29.

[2] Champlain, *Voyages*, Laverdières ed., p. 562.

[3] *Jesuit Relations*, R. G. Thwaites ed., vol. XVII, p. 271, explanatory note 9.

[4] Lafitau, *Moeurs des Sauvages Ameriquains*, pt. II, p. 13.

Cf. Champlain, *Voyages*, Prince Soc. ed., vol. III, pp. 160, 161.

of the winter. These are great holes in the ground, four or five feet deep, lined with pieces of bark inside and covered over with earth.

"As to the corn, instead of burying it, except in case of necessity, they dry it on long poles, and upon the porches or exterior vestibules of the cabins. At tsonnontouann they make granaries of bark in the form of towers, on high ground, and they pierce the bark on all sides, to allow the air to penetrate and prevent the grain from moulding." The corn was first dried in the cabins "on poles running across, which are arranged around the fire, and which rest upon the posts which support the structure; the smoke which is produced day and night blackens the grain a little after a while, but removes any moisture which might spoil it. In winter, when it is thoroughly dry, they shell it, and put it into the great casks of bark. . . and they take from these as required. They leave in the smoke only that which they reserve for seed, and which they shell only when it is time for planting."[1]

Morgan makes the following reference to granaries and storage pits: "The Iroquois were accustomed to bury their surplus corn and also their charred green corn in caches, in which the former would preserve uninjured through the year, and the latter for a much longer period. They excavated a pit, made a bark bottom and sides, and having deposited their corn within it, a bark roof, water tight, was constructed over it, and the whole covered with earth. Pits of charred corn are still found near their ancient settlements."[2]

The storage of corn in pits is no longer practised, though potatoes, carrots, and other vegetables, also squashes and pumpkins, are frequently stored in this way (Plate X). The pits are made by digging rather large holes, lining these with various materials, such as straw or boards, and finally covering them over with earth to a depth which will exclude the frost. In

---

[1] Lafitau, *Moeurs des Sauvages Ameriquains*, vol. II, pp. 79, 80.

[2] Morgan, *League of the Iroquois*, p. 311.

Hennepin, *A New Discovery*, R. G. Thwaites ed., vol. I, p. 46, states of the Seneca that they store their corn "into Caves digged in the Earth, and cover'd after such a manner. that no Rain can come at it."

the absence of other materials, hemlock boughs may be used, sometimes with the addition of a layer of bark. Onondaga informants at Grand River reserve stated that several of the larger species of carex were formerly used, to which the general name of uhee˞gwa' is given, also meadow foxtail or udę'´ę'.[1] Many of the pits found in the Iroquois country contain both charred grain and portions of the carbonized lining of grass or hemlock boughs. For squashes, etc., the leaves of the sumac, utgo'´da', are said to answer very well. A general name given for pit is watsha'dǫ'. A potato pit is called ononu˞gwa' watsha'dǫ'.

Champlain is probably the first explorer to describe the pit method of storage, which he observed among some of the eastern Algonkin. Trenches were excavated to a depth of 5 or 6 feet on a dry, sandy slope and the grain, in grass sacks, covered over 3 or 4 feet deep with sand.[2] Kalm, with reference to eastern North America, remarks that "they dug these holes seldom deeper than a fathom, and often not so deep; at the bottom and on the sides they put broad pieces of bark. The Andropogon bicorne . . . supplies the want of bark; the ears of maize are then thrown into the hole and covered to a considerable thickness with the same grass, and the whole is again covered by a sufficient quantity of earth."[3]

ABNORMAL EARS.[4]

Abnormal ears of various kinds are frequently found and are usually considered significant.[5]

A smutty ear is called in Onondaga odjiigwą̈'daa', which means a rotten body. A Seneca name obtained was utgęs one'ǫ', which signifies rotten corn.

A fasciated ear, sometimes more or less palmate, with branches resembling fingers, is called in Onondaga o'´nia' unę'ha', or hand corn.

---

[1] Peter John, John Jamieson, and others.

[2] Pinkerton, *Voyages and Travels*, vol. 12, p. 258. "The Indians thrash it as they gather it. They dry it well on matts in the sun, and bury it in holes in the ground, lined with moss or matts, which are their barns."

[3] *Kalm's Travels*, vol. II, p. 115.

[4] Peter John and others.

[5] See also Parker, *Bulletin 144, New York State Museum*, p. 33.

A multiple ear, taking the form of a large ear with several smaller ones springing from it, indicates that a girl will have many children. The rest of the huskers say "uiäga'ʼdιʻ" (On.), or "lots of young ones."

A bifurcated ear, having two or three rows on opposite sides and none between, is o'naʼʻsa', or tongue, in Onondaga. In Mohawk this is called yuhaʼdι' oʼnαstι', or road corn. A girl must not eat this, otherwise an enemy would find the way to her without fail. When any one discovers such an ear, the others all contribute an ear to his or her pile of husked corn.

A nubbin, or short ear, is called udnoia'ʼgiʻ, which means that the husks have all been removed. The ear is considered unfit for braiding and is merely thrown on the floor to dry.

A cob with no corn on it is called odji'swą̈' (On.), a name indicating simply the absence of kernels.

When any of the huskers finds a stray red or coloured ear, the others also contribute to his or her pile. The name applied to such an ear is deyudji'doʼʻyeʻ (On.), which is descriptive of the variegated colouring.

Sometimes a podded grain is found on an ordinary ear. A grain of this kind is immediately swallowed as a means of securing prosperity in any enterprise, such as marriage or hunting.

When corn hybridizes from being too near another variety, the hybrid ears are called odinada'ʼhą̈' onęʼha' (On.), or visitor corn.

A corn plant producing white leaves is called the old one or the grandmother of the lot, etiʼsoʼdaʻ (On.).

It was remarked by David Jack that in his younger days when a husking bee was held, the workers were always on the look-out for abnormal ears. A red ear entitled the finder to one ear from each of the others; an ear with one or more rows missing, to two ears all around; an ear with no corn at all on it, to one ear; a fasciated ear, to five ears. A kind of divination with corn ears, according to John Jamieson, jun., and John Echo, is sometimes practised as follows: a few grains are placed inside a weasel-skin, the whole is placed in water over night, then planted, some native tobacco being placed with it and an invocation being made asking for power for the medicine which is to be made in this way and stating what it is wanted for. When the corn grows and forms ears, one of these is taken, preferably one which forms abnormally among the anthers or parts of the tassel at the end of the stalk. This ear is then used by the person (who is usually a medicine-man or woman) for divining the appropriate remedies in cases of sickness. To do this, some article of clothing belonging to the sick person is wrapped about the ear of corn, the whole being placed under the medicine-man's pillow to dream upon.

A cob of the kind just described may also be kept for luck in hunting, or may be simply preserved for future use in divination. The idea of sympathetic magic is involved in the foregoing procedure, the weasel being considered to have a "good head."

COOKERY AND EATING CUSTOMS.

EATING CUSTOMS.

One regular meal per day seems to have been the rule, although early writers record the preparation of two meals among the Huron.[1] An Onondaga informant remembers when some of the older people had no regular meal-time. Members of the family ate whenever they felt like it. A big bowl of soup, however, was cooked in the morning. They usually worked for a while, then came in and ate the soup or corn bread.[2] Breakfast is called in Onondaga hặigeⁿ djᵢkga'kwa', or "morning meal." A meal partaken of in the evening is oga'sɑ'ga'kwa'. Nowadays dinner, gặihia'hega'kwa', is added.

The meal is usually announced by the woman of the house, who calls, "hauo'nɛ, sɛdeko'nia' (On.)," or "all right, come and eat." The men, as a rule, are helped first, the women and children coming after. The serving in former times was done directly from the pot into bark or wooden dishes, chunks of

[1] Champlain, *Voyages*, vol. III, p. 164.

Jesuit Relations, R. G. Thwaites ed., vol. VIII, p. 111.

[2] This item is confirmed by Morgan, *Houses and House Life of the American Aborigines*, p. 99.

Informants: Peter John, Jairus Pierce, and others.

meat being handed or tossed to those desiring a portion. Some of the older people at Onondaga Castle and elsewhere remember when meals were served in this way. Wooden spoons or ladles, some of considerable size, were used for dipping and eating liquid foods. These are mentioned frequently by early historians, also the fact that each guest, upon being invited to a feast, was expected to bring his own dish and spoon. Wooden eating spoons are seldom used nowadays, although the old-fashioned dipping ladles may sometimes be seen at longhouse ceremonies.

Each one ate in silence, either sitting or standing, the only convenience being the bare ground or the edge of the sleeping platform. It is at present considered etiquette for a guest, in finishing, to say "nia'wę" (On.), or "thanks." To this the host replies, "niuⁿ," "It is well." Children are told that a failure to say nia'wę or thank you will give them a stomach-ache. Any one coming in at meal-time is invited to eat and is expected as a matter of etiquette to take something.

A joke or witticism is sometimes made at the expense of the women when a meal is unduly delayed. This is to the effect that a number of people were seen coming along the road reduced to skeletons, or "all bones." The explanation is that this was caused by starvation, to which the narrators were also exposed by having to wait so long for dinner or supper.

Cleanliness, from a European point of view, was not always a desideratum in earlier times. Graphic descriptions are furnished by the missionaries of the incrustation of food inside the pots and the general carelessness in cooking. Fresh meat became coated with hairs and dirt. The dogs fought for a share and constant watchfulness was necessitated to prevent one's food from being snatched away. Grease was wiped upon the clothing, the hair, or upon the dogs. Informants at Grand River, Tonawanda, and elsewhere mentioned the use of rotten pine or chestnut for the absorption of grease or perspiration, or for dusting babies.[1] This is made into a fine dark red powder. A Mohawk name for the material is oheⁿsa'.

A belief noted at Oneidatown, Ontario, is that food dropped during a meal must not be picked up, as this is for the dead.

---

[1] *Jesuit Relations*, R. G. Thwaites ed., vol. I, p. 285; also vol. V, p. 103.

If picked up, it must be laid to one side.[1] The functions of the U'gi'we society, in fact, are based upon the belief that the dead suffer from hunger and require satisfaction at intervals. Neglect in this respect is followed by continued visitations and ultimate illness.

Smoking followed eating, perhaps more especially on occasions of ceremony.[2]

Terms Used in Connexion with Eating.[3]

Good appetite, ekwanǫ'wɑks.
I am hungry, ɑksis.
Glutton, sadetcą' or sasą"gwą.
I eat, waga'deko'nia'.
You eat, wa'sadeko'nia'.
He eats, hodekoni'.
She eats, godeko'ni'.
Oven, untä'go'ndakwa'gı'.
Bread-pan, untä'go'ndakwa'.

HOUSEHOLD CONVENIENCES.

A characteristic feature of early Iroquois architecture was the long communal cabin, constructed usually of elm bark and accomodating a number of families. Champlain gives the following general description: "Their cabins are in the shape of tunnels or arbors, and are covered with the bark of trees. They are from twenty-five to thirty fathoms long, more or less, and six wide, having a passageway through the middle from ten to twelve feet wide, which extends from one end to the other. On the two sides there is a kind of bench, four feet high, where they sleep in the summer, in order to avoid the annoyance of the fleas. . . In winter they sleep on the ground on mats near the fire. . . . They lay up a stock of dry wood, with which they fill their cabins, to burn in winter. At the extremity of the cabins there is a space, where they preserve their Indian

---

[1] Mrs. David Williams.
[2] *Jesuit Relations*, R. G. Thwaites ed., vol. XXVII, p. 249.
[3] These are in Onondaga.

corn, which they put into great casks made of the bark of trees. They have pieces of wood suspended, on which they put their clothes, provisions, and other things, for fear of the mice, of which there are great numbers. In one of these cabins there may be twelve fires, and twenty-four families. It smokes excessively, from which it follows that many receive serious injury to the eyes. . . . There is no window nor any opening, except that in the upper part of their cabins for the smoke to escape."[1] Sagard, who gives a similar description, refers to the porches which were constructed at either end of the cabins, and which served for the storage of corn, etc. Very few aboriginal features are seen in present-day houses (Plate XI), though poles are still suspended above the fire for drying clothing and various articles of food.[2]

GENERAL CHARACTERISTICS.

The general improvidence ascribed to many of the eastern tribes is evidently inapplicable to the Iroquois proper, though all Iroquoian tribes were possibly not so provident. Lafitau, for instance, remarks of the Hurons that "necessity, to which they are often reduced by this sort of liberality, obliges them to eat everything and to enjoy the fare. As, in their times of plenty, they allow no time for meat to spoil, placing it still alive in the pot, or roasting and turning it on little spits of wood, one end of which they stick in the ground, so they do not hesitate to eat stinking and almost rotten meat when they have no other. They never skim the pot, in order to lose nothing. They cook frogs whole and swallow them without disgust. They dry the intestines of deer without cleaning them and find them as tasty as we find woodcock. . . They have not abandoned the acorn. . They gather beech-nuts with care and crush them. They eat potatoes with pleasure, various insipid roots, and all sorts of wild and bitter fruits; they give these no time to ripen

---

[1] Champlain, Prince Society ed., vol. III, pp. 160, 161.
[2] Sagard says: "In the centre of their dwellings there are two great poles suspended, which they call ouaronta, from which they hang their pot-hooks, their clothing, provisions and other things to protect them from mice, as well as to dry them."—*Voyage*, vol. I, p. 83.

and to grow, for fear that others might gather them first. In order the better to despoil a tree they cut it down at the root, without worrying about the advantages they might derive in succeeding years."[1]

A most important factor in food preparation was the production of fire. In more ancient times this was produced by friction. Among the methods in vogue among the Iroquois were:

Flint and pyrites.[2]

A fire-drill consisting of a simple spindle twirled between the hands.

The pump drill, in which the spindle was given momentum by means of a spindle-whorl of wood.

The bow drill, in which the spindle was operated by a bow, the string of which was twisted once around the spindle (Plate XII).

The fire plow, in which the end of a stick was rubbed vigorously back and forth in a groove.

The fire saw, in which one stick was rubbed across another.

Of these, the flint and pyrites, pump drill, bow drill, fire plow, and fire saw are said to have been used within the recollection of some of the older people. The fact of such a variety of methods being found in use contemporaneously evidently denotes accultural influences. The pump drill was quite commonly employed in the production of "new fire" at the New Year Festival, also in the Sun Ceremony.[3] This implement

---

[1] Lafitau, *Moeurs des Sauvages*, pt. II, pp. 91, 92.

Jesuit Relations, R. G. Thwaites ed., vol. XXIII, pp. 63, 65.

[2] Le Jeune, in describing the fire-making methods of the Montagnais, states that "they strike together two metallic stones. . . . in place of matches, they use a little piece of tinder, a dry and rotten wood . . . when they have lighted it, they put it into pulverized cedar bark; and, by gently blowing, this bark takes fire."—*Jesuit Relations*, R. G. Thwaites ed., vol. VI, p. 217.

[3] Prevailed among Iroquois and Algonkin families north of the Ohio; extended west of the Mississippi, and was in all cases attended with ceremonies, though not observed in the more northerly regions with as much

consisted of a spindle with a disk of wood; a cross-piece, to the ends of which a slack cord was attached, the centre of the cord being fastened to the top of the spindle; and lastly, a hearth of dry wood for drilling upon. The drill was operated by giving the cord a few twists around the spindle, then alternately pressing downward and relaxing the pressure, which caused the spindle to revolve rapidly in a small depression at one side of the hearth. A small groove at one side of this allowed the ignited dust to fall upon some tinder placed below[1]; a socket was sometimes applied to the top of the spindle to increase the pressure.

Hennepin, in speaking of the fire-making methods of the Illinois and neighbouring tribes, states that a stick or spindle of some hard wood was used upon a hearth of cedar; this was the spindle twirled between the hands.[2] The same method was employed by the Huron,[3] as well as by many other tribes through-

---

solemnity as in the Gulf State region.—See Schoolcraft, *Indian Tribes of U.S.*, vol. V, p. 104.

Cf. Brinton, *Myths of the New World*, p. 183, regarding mythical origin of fire.

[1] Morgan, *League of the Iroquois*, vol. II, p. 39.

[2] Hennepin, *A New Discovery*, R. G. Thwaites ed., vol. I, p. 246; Loskiel, pt. I, p. 54.

[3] Le Jeune remarks, with regard to the Montagnais and more particularly to the Hurons: "They have still another kind of fuse. They twist a little cedar stick, and this friction causes fire, which lights some tinder."—*Jesuit Relations*, R. G. Thwaites ed., VI, p. 267.

Sagard gives the Huron method in detail: "They take two sticks of willow, basswood, or some other kind, dry and light, then arrange two sticks of willow, basswood, or some other kind, dry and light, then arranging one about the length of the forearm or less, and of the thickness of the finger, and having along the side a small hole about the size of a knife point or a beaver's tooth, and a little groove with a notch at one side, to allow to fall upon some tinder placed below the powder which is brought to ignition. They place the point of another stick of the same wood, and as large as the little finger or less, in the hole thus commenced and turn this in the hands so vigorously and so long that they light the tinder, and then with some small, dry sticks they kindle a fire for cooking. All wood, however, is not suitable for making fire. . . . At times, when they have difficulty, they powder up in the hole a little charcoal or a little dry powdered wood which they get from some stump; if they have no large stick (for a hearth) they take two round ones, tie them together

out the continent. A Cayuga informant[1] gives, as the best materials for spindles, the wood of the slippery elm and the hickory, with a hearth of basswood, maple, or any hard wood. Among the materials used by Tonawanda fire-makers[2] for the same purpose, were slippery elm and white ash, with a hearth of dry basswood. Ironwood was employed for both spindles and hearths by the Onondaga and others. Button-wood is also mentioned as a spindle material. Chief Gibson described a drill in which the spindle was of hickory and the hearth of pitch pine.

A Cayuga informant[3] remembered the use of an unusual form of pump drill, in which the spindle was over 4 feet in length, a comparatively small whorl being required, owing to the weight of the spindle (Plate XIII). It was also stated that in olden times the whorl or disk was made of a small branch bent into a circle and interlaced with bark.[4] The whorl is considered to be better a little out of centre to ensure greater friction.

The fire plow was also in use among the Onondaga, though more rarely employed.

The fire saw method was described by John Jamieson, jun. A fallen ironwood tree is found and a dry spot in it is selected. A stick of the same wood is cut and is rubbed back and forth across the log by two persons. The tinder mentioned was the *Polporus applanatus* fungus (Unä'sa'), dried and shredded.

The bow drill, as used at Tonawanda, consisted of a spindle of white ash or slippery elm, with a hearth of dry basswood. The string for the bow was the inner bark of the moose or leatherwood. The punk was described as rotten maple, prepared for

---

by their ends, and placing the knee upon them to hold them, place between them the point of another stick made like a weaver's shuttle, and whirl this by the other end between the hands, as before."—*Voyage*, I, pp. 48, 49.

H. S. Caswell, *Our Life Among the Iroquois*, p. 237: fire-making by twirling a stick between the hands is described by Squire Johnson as an old Iroquois method.

[1] John Jamieson, jun.
[2] Alex. Snider.
[3] Bob Smoke.
[4] John Jamieson, jun.

use by drying. Other kinds of punk mentioned were: beech rot, dried; a species of *Polyporus*[1] found growing on pines; fat pine, slivered up small; also dry hemlock twigs. These were packed closely around the base of the drill and kindled into a fire by blowing.

Among the European methods used later were: the flint and steel, and the burning glass, both of which were articles of trade in early days. The inflammability of the wadding used in the old-fashioned muzzle-loaders was noted and fire was frequently kindled by setting off a charge of powder.

Terms Used in Fire-making (On.).

Fire-drill, edjisdonia'̓ta'.
Spindle, gaią̈du'da'.
Whorl, dewa'ci'̓dǫ'da˄gwi'.
Cross-piece, ganą̈tcu'da'gwɩ' or degayadǫ'da'gwɩ'.
Rock used for making fire, deyedji'sdae'sta' ustą̈'hä' (to make fire-rock).
Flint, uhω'ɛ'.
New fire, udjisda'se'.
Pitch pine, ushe'sdaa' or ushe'sdada'.
Punk, unä'sa' (Ca. unra'̓sa').
He makes fire with a drill, ą̈hadjisdo·'̓nia'.

THE GATHERING OF WOOD.

The provision of firewood was evidently as much a problem in former times as now, and village sites were frequently changed, at least partly, on this account.[2] Sagard informs us that "they

---

[1] *Polyporus igniarius* (or *Fomes igniarius*).

[2] Loskiel, pt. I, pp. 55, 56: "They never think of sparing the forest trees, for they not only burn more wood than is necessary for house consumption, but destroy them by peeling. The greatest havoc among the forest trees is made by fires, which happen either accidentally, or are kindled by the Indians, who in spring, and sometimes in autumn, burn the withered grass, that a fresh crop may grow for the deer. These fires run on for many miles, burning the bark at the roots of the trees in such a manner, that they die. A forest of fir trees is in general destroyed by these fires.

"From these and other causes, the fire-wood at last begins to be scarce, and necessity obliges them to seek other dwelling-places."

fill with dry wood for winter use all the space beneath the platforms, which they call garihagueu and eindichaguet; but the big trunks or logs, which serve to hold the fire, raised a little at one end, they pile in front of their cabins, or store them in the entries, which they call aque. All the women assist in providing wood, which begins with the months of March and April. They use only good wood, preferring to go far for it rather than to use green or smoky fuel. If they do not find perfectly dry trees, they fell those having dry branches, which they break into splinters and cut an equal length. They do not use fagots nor the very large trunks, which they allow to lie and rot, as they have no saws to saw them."[1]

A social custom which was frequently practised by the women was the providing of the winter's supply of firewood for brides who were married too late in the season to undertake this duty for themselves. In Sagard's vocabulary of the Huron language an allusion is found to the cry which was uttered through the village by the crier, calling upon all the wood-gatherers to go to the forest to collect the general supply. This was escoirhaykion! escoirhaykion! (To the forest! To the forest!).

The gathering of wood is still very often done by the women, and by the older men, who sometimes employ the pack-basket (Plate XIV, fig. a), or the hand-sleigh, for transportation.

UTENSILS USED IN THE GATHERING, PREPARATION, AND EATING OF FOOD.

COOKING METHODS AND UTENSILS.

Cookery methods, generally speaking, have evidently undergone considerable change, more particularly during the historical period. Not only were there modifications in fire-making, but also in the utensils employed, the changes in the latter being probably the most important. Lafitau remarks of this that "before the Europeans brought them kettles or pots from across the ocean they (the women) made use of earthen vessels, which they manufactured with some skill, giving them a spherical form at the bottom and considerable width at the

---

[1] Sagard, *Voyage*, I, p. 82.

top; and after having dried them in the sun, they burnt them in a slow fire made with bark. The more migratory tribes possessed only wooden cooking utensils, less fragile, but easier of transportation. They cooked their food in these by throwing into the water, one after the other, heated stones. This gradually heated the water, and caused it to boil sufficiently to satisfy people who were accustomed to partly-cooked food."[1] Bressani comments on a lack of suitable cooking appliances among the Hurons: "Before knowing the Europeans, as they had no kettles for cooking victuals, especially on their journeys, they made a ditch in the earth, and filled it with water, which they caused to boil by cooling in it a number of stones, first heated red-hot for this purpose."[2] The inference is that this was a hasty method employed when the ordinary utensils were not at hand.

Informants at Grand River and elsewhere state that boiling was sometimes practised by placing a bark vessel in direct contact with the fire, a fact which is confirmed by historical references. Squire Johnson, an aged Seneca, remarks that "they cooked their meat in a bark kettle, which they made by using a flint axe or chisel to separate the bark from an elm tree. They tied the large pieces of bark together at the ends with strips of the inner bark, making a dish large enough to hold the meat, with water enough to boil it. This bark kettle was suspended between two sticks over the fire, and before the kettle was burnt through the meat was cooked."[3] It is said that by protecting the edges of the vessel from the flames it answered this purpose very well.

While the greater part of the foods used by the Iroquois seems to have been prepared by boiling, such methods as baking on a flat stone[4], roasting or cooking in the red-hot embers and broiling on spits or sticks stuck into the ground before the fire,

---

[1] Lafitau, *Moeurs*, vol. II, p. 87.
Cf. *Jesuit Relations*, R. G. Thwaites ed., vol. I, p. 285.
[2] *Jesuit Relations*, R. G. Thwaites ed., vol. XXXVIII, p. 255.
[3] Caswell, H. S., *Our Life Among the Iroquois*, pp. 237, 238.
[4] Adair, *Hist. of the North American Indians*, pp. 407, 408.
This method is still remembered by some of the older people.

were also extensively practised. Pits of suitable size were frequently dug in the side of some convenient bank or clay deposit. A fire was built in these, the coals removed, and corn, squashes, roots, and other foods baked by covering over with ashes. Archæological remains of such pits are common.

The use of earthenware pots in the boiling of meat, etc., is attested by many early writers and observers, and is further suggested by the form of the utensils found and the evident employment of many of them in cooking operations as indicated by thei nterior incrustations.

The rounded bottoms were evidently adapted equally for standing in the light soil, which usually formed the floors of the cabins, or for maintaining an upright position in the fire, the latter of which is suggested by such illustrations as those of Lafitau[1] and others.

The extension rim found on most of the pots, suggests that they could have been tied about the neck with bark cord or vines and suspended from poles arranged either tripod-fashion, or between crotches. Schoolcraft figures an arrangement of this kind.[2]

The introduction of the European pot or kettle not only increased the facilities for preparing food, but was both more economical and convenient than its predecessors, one of the immediate results being that the making of pottery was discontinued, perhaps gradually at first, but so completely in most cases that no recollection remains of its method of manufacture, though a number of more or less complete descriptions are given by various writers.[3]

The kettles obtained in trade were mostly of copper and brass, though cast-iron seems also to have been in vogue to

---

[1] Lafitau, *Moeurs*, II, plate V, fig. 1.
Beverly, *Hist. of Virginia*, see plate.
White, John, *Roanoke Colony*, 1585-88.

[2] Schoolcraft, *Historical and Statistical Information*, pt. I, plate XXII.

[3] Sagard, *Voyages*, I, p. 99. Also *Histoire du Canada*, Tross ed., p. 260.
Holmes, 20th Ann. Rep. B.A.E., *Aboriginal Pottery of the Eastern United States*, pp. 1-201.
Cushing, F. H., *The Germ of Shoreland Pottery*, Memoirs Inter. Congress of Anthrop., Chicago, 1894.

some extent, and small pots of the latter material have been preserved by some as relics of these earlier times. The iron pot is most frequently used at present.

Fire and Cookery Terms (Onondaga).

Fire, ode′ka'.
Ashes, ogę′hε'.
Firewood, oyä′da'.
Charcoal or coal, uswä′da' (something black).
Smoke, oyę″gwaa'.
Smoke coming out of a chimney, oyę‘ gwae′da'.
Blaze or flames, o'dǫ″gwa'.
Match, dega'da′kwa.'
I make a fire, gadega″ta'.
She makes a fire, ǫdega″ta'.
He makes a fire, hadega″ta'.
Pole for suspending a pot, o'ä′na'.
Crotch used in suspension of pole, ga‘sa′ε'.
Pothook (of wood), ga‘su″daa'.
Large pot, gana'dju′wa′neꞌ.
Brass kettle, ga‘na'dji‘aǫ′wıꞌ.
Small pot (iron), nigana″djiaaꞌ.
Boiling, o·ya′hä̧s.
Cooking, goko′niꞌ.
One who cooks, ekonia′ha'.
Roasting in a pan, wade″skǫ′da' ǫde'skǫda″kwa'gıꞌ.
Frying-pan, ǫde″skǫda′kwa'.

An interesting enumeration of cooking methods and utensils is given by Mary Jemison: "Our cooking consisted in pounding our corn into samp or hominy, boiling the hominy, making now and then a cake and baking it in the ashes, and in boiling and roasting our venison. As our cooking and eating utensils consisted of a hommany block and pestle, a small kettle, a knife or two, and a few vessels of bark or wood, it required but little time to keep them in order for use."[1]

---

[1] Seaver, *Life of Mrs. Mary Jemison*, p. 43.

MORTARS AND PESTLES.

Quite a number of Indian families still retain the corn mortar (Plate XVIII), or "hommany block" referred to by Mary Jemison. This may usually be seen standing upsidedown just outside the door, and is very frequently made of the black, red, or other varieties of oak, and the pestle of maple, ironwood, ash, or hickory. Buttonwood was mentioned by a Tonawanda informant as a suitable mortar material. Elm is also used at times, but is not considered as good.

In the manufacture of the mortar, a tree of suitable dimensions is felled and allowed to lie until it becomes properly seasoned. A block or section is then cut off pretty well up the trunk where the diameter is most uniform. A number of inquiries and measurements made indicate that the height is made to conform with the convenience of the user or owner. A hemispherical or slightly conical hollow is next excavated in one end of the block by burning and then hacking or scraping away the burnt material. The depth of the hollow varies somewhat, but is usually from 8 to 12 inches.

The pestle is double-ended, with a place for grasping the centre, though only one end is used until this becomes worn or broken, the purpose of the opposite end being principally to give weight and balance.

The pestle is grasped firmly in both hands and brought down smartly, a few minutes vigorous pounding being sufficient to produce meal for a batch of bread or hominy. Anywhere from one to four people may pound at once, the pestles being brought down alternately or one after the other.

A peculiar circular scraping or rubbing motion is imparted to the pestle from time to time, the object being to dislodge the meal which adheres to the sides of the mortar. This rather difficult feat is accomplished without losing a stroke.

Some of the older people relate how the women of neighbouring houses sometimes ran races to see who could perform the operations of grinding and making the meal into cakes most quickly.

A Mohawk informant describes a taboo to the effect that a woman at the monthly period should be prohibited from pounding corn, also from touching foods or medicine. Illness of various kinds is ascribed to neglect of this precaution.[1] An Onondaga informant held that no harm would result so long as the woman is not allowed to touch the corn.

If a woman at this period, according to David Key (On.), prepares food for twins, the latter will no longer be able to foretell future events or perform the other remarkable things attributed to them.

In former times, when a girl arrived at puberty, waǫdodia'ga' (On.), her parents or relatives gathered up a quantity of the hardest corn they could find, selecting sweet corn, if they could get it, as being the hardest to grind into meal. More than enough for a day's grinding was prepared and the unsuspecting maiden was required to perform the task in a single day. If she were successful, it was regarded as a sign that she would be an industrious housewife. If a mortar or the corn were not available, she was set at cutting down a tree with a dull axe.[2] Puberty customs of this kind are still practised by the more conservative.

The wooden mortar, with comparatively little variation of form, is widely distributed throughout the various regions of corn culture. The pestles, also, exhibit some similarity, though those employed by some tribes show no particular attempt at working into shape.

A very crude or primitive method of grinding corn was by means of two medium-sized pebbles of a flat-round shape, the lower one pitted slightly in the centre to hold the grains (Plate XIV, fig. c).

A slightly varying form consists of a muller for holding in one hand and a shallow mortar or mealing slab, an outfit which could be readily carried (Plate XIV, fig. d). Mullers and mealing slabs of this variety are occasionally found near old cabin sites on the present reservations. An earlier form of this device may be represented by the depressions found on the flattened surfaces of large rocks and boulders. A considerable number of the latter have been found in Iroquois territory.

---

[1] Seth Newhouse (Mo.), Canienga, Brant County reserve.
[2] John Jamieson, jun.

Cylindrical pestles of stone were evidently not in use among the Iroquois, though employed by their Algonkin neighbours to the east as late as the Revolutionary war.[1]

The use of flattened pebbles for cracking corn and nuts is still remembered by quite a number of the older people, and is mentioned frequently in the Relations and elsewhere as a convenient or auxiliary method among the Hurons and Iroquois generally and many of the surrounding tribes. A couple of stones of this kind were obtained from an Indian family at Caughnawaga. Mrs. J. Williams of the same village remembers that about fifty years ago corn was often ground by taking two pebbles, as described, one usually somewhat larger than the other; the larger was placed in a large wooden bowl held in the lap and the grain either cracked, or ground into a meal (Plate XV).

David Jack, of the Grand River reserve, was of the opinion that the wooden mortar as now used is not an extremely old device with the Iroquois, though Lafitau figures a mortar of this kind at an early date. It was stated by Jack that the older people used sometimes to burn a hole in the trunk of a fallen tree, a device suggestive of that in use among the Ojibwa, Pottawatomie, Seminoles, and others, the pounder or pestle in the latter instance being simply a large hardwood stick.[2]

Onondaga and Mohawk Terms.

Wooden mortar, ga'niga˄da' ga'ni˄ga' (Mo.).
Stone mortar or mealing slab, onä'ya' (a stone).
Muller, deyenɛhia'kta' onɛ'ha' (cracker for corn).
She is cracking corn, deyenɛ'hiaks onɛ'ha'.
She is pounding corn (in the mortar), ete''tha'.
Pestle, ga'niga˄da' hıʹtgäka', mill or mortar the top ones
    aʻsi'zaʻ eyɛda'kwa' (Mo.).
Two women are pounding corn, genithe'ta' (Mo.).

---

[1] One of these was found in the Rideau valley by Dr. T. W. Beeman; see *Ontario Arch. Rep., 1904*, p. 17.

[2] For bibliography, etc., see *Handbook of American Indians*, vol. I, pp. 954. 955.

Several women are pounding corn, gondithe'ta' (Mo.).
She is pounding corn, yithe'ta' (Mo.).

THE PACK BASKET—YαNTαSHAGE″DαSTA' (SEN.)[1]

The pack or carrying basket (Plates XX, XXII, fig. e) had a variety of uses. It is still frequently employed during harvest for gathering corn, and sometimes for carrying the smaller children. It also formed a convenient receptacle for collecting firewood, or for the transportation of provisions. Those used for corn or wood are very strongly made. A burden strap or tump line, gαsha'a' (Sen.), is attached for carrying.

Indications are frequently found suggesting an improvement and an extension of basket-making with the introduction of European tools, and the pack basket has no doubt also undergone some changes, though there is little variety of form to be found at present. A specimen differing somewhat from the ordinary type was collected at Oneidatown, Ontario. This was concaved on one side to fit the shoulders, and was said to be an old Oneida style (Plate XXI).

The favourite Iroquois basketry material everywhere is black ash. The tree is cut into logs some 6 or 8 feet in length, the bark is removed and the outside pounded with the back of an axe or with a mallet, until the layers can be separated into strips. When black ash cannot be found, other woods, such as hickory, soft maple, and birch, are made use of in the same way. Another material which was sometimes pressed into service for the manufacture of pack baskets was the bark stripped from young hickories (Plate XIV, fig. b).

HULLING OR WASHING BASKET—YEGAI″DOÄ″TA' (SEN.).[2]

The hulling or washing basket is always twilled, the sides being woven tightly and the bottoms made open and sieve-like.

---

[1] The ordinary Seneca word for basket is ga'αshä'.
Onondaga names given for corn carrying basket are:
    enähanę'gwi″ta' ga'a″sää' or
    egehä′ạda″kwa' ga'a″sää'.
[2] An Onondaga name is ɩnähuhai′i'ta' ga'a″sää', "washing corn basket."
The operation of washing the corn in the basket is referred to as e′nähuhai′i'nɩ'.

There is some variation in size to correspond with family requirements; otherwise there is little difference, except with regard to the handle. One style of basket has none; another has an opening on each side for the hands immediately below the rim; a third has only one such opening;[1] a fourth has small bent wooden handles inserted on opposite sides, while a fifth has a wooden handle extending from side to side. Black ash splints are the ordinary material (Plate XXII, figs. a, c, d).

A flexible washing basket is used on several of the reservations. This is constructed of basswood inner bark or bast, in an open hexagonal weave like snowshoe netting (Plate XXII, fig. b).

The ripe corn is usually hulled for cookery purposes. The first step in hulling is to add sifted hardwood ashes to a pot of water in the proportion of about one double handful to three quarts of water. This is brought to a boil to dissolve the lye. The strength of the solution is tested by tasting. The corn, previously boiled a little to soften it, is then added and boiled until it begins to look swollen. The principal test, however, is the slipping of the skin when a grain is pressed between the fingers. The corn and ashes are stirred from time to time while the boiling is in progress; the cobs are thrown into the fire as fuel. The contents of the pot are next emptied into the washing basket, allowed to drain a little, then soused and shaken about with a whirling motion in several tubs or kettles of water, or in a running stream, until the hulls have been rubbed off and floated away, a process which is assisted by friction against the twilled sides of the basket and by rubbing with the hands.

The corn is now ready to pound, if required for breadmaking, or for use whole in hulled corn soup, a very popular food. Another rapid boiling and washing are often given to remove all traces of lye.

The following terms are applied to hulled corn:

gageʻhoʻtcų (On.), the skins off.

gançhuhaiʻt (On.), corn washed with water.

---

[1] Peter John (On.) thinks this the oldest style.

THE SIFTING BASKET.

Sifters differ but little except in fineness. These are twilled and sometimes reinforced around the bottoms (Plate XXIII, figs, b, c.).

The finest are for the preparation of the meal for corn bread. The Seneca term for a basket of this sort is niyuᵛniyuᵛsda'sa'a.

The hominy sifter, u'nę'yusdowanes (Sen.)[1], is somewhat coarser, as indicated by the name. A common size is about a foot square at the top and tapering slightly towards the bottom. The larger particles are again pounded until all are of the requisite size.

A special basket is said to have formerly been employed for sifting ashes. At present, however, the ordinary type of fine sifter is used, most frequently one which has become somewhat old or worn.

That sifters of other materials and patterns were sometimes used is indicated by historical references. One writer remarks of a mixed band of Senecas, Oneidas, Mohawks, and Wyandots, who resided in Ohio in the early part of the nineteenth century, that "sometimes they pounded the corn and sifted it through a skin with holes punched in it and made bread, and boiled the coarser for hominy."[2]

The suggestion of evolution in basketry is further confirmed by such references as the following from Lafitau, who remarks that the sieve was not basket-like then, but was a flat, rectangular article, "coarsely made, of small branches tied together." He further states that grain was winnowed in bark vessels or in pliable baskets made of rushes (jonc).[3]

A very old and battered flour-sifter, collected at Caughnawaga, was made of slender splinters of hickory in a sort of wicker weave. The splints were interlaced and also bound at the top with hickory bark, the whole forming a deep and rather

---

[1] An Onondaga name is unisdu'wanɛ's ųwa'kta', or large particles sifter. The fine sifter is called ųwa'kta'.

[2] *Western Reserve Hist. Soc. Tracts*, No. 64, p. 106.

[3] Lafitau, *Moeurs*, vol. II, p. 86.

flat receptable. An old type of popcorn sifter is figured by Morgan,[1] which is woven in a similar manner (Plate XXIII, fig. a).

BREAD BOWLS (BARK AND WOOD).

It seems probable that bark was formerly even more popular than wood in the manufacture of household utensils. The material was found in abundance and could soon be worked into shape. Bark is still used occasionally for utensils, and many of the older people remember when it was quite extensively employed.

Large bowls for bread-making were frequently made of elm bark. The latter was removed from the tree in the spring or early summer when the sap is up. It was then bent into shape and the edges strengthened with strips of hickory or other material, which was bound into position with the inner bark of the elm or basswood. A couple of specimens in the Victoria Memorial Museum at Ottawa are nearly 2 feet in diameter and 7 or 8 inches deep (Plate XXIV, fig. c).

Such bowls were also employed for other purposes than the making of bread. A Caughnawaga informant states that they were frequently used for holding the stones for cracking corn on the lap (Plate XV). They also answered as dish pans, wash pans, for holding food, and as general culinary utensils. The usual form was round, though some are oval or of an oblong rectangular shape.

Bark is mentioned repeatedly by all the early writers as the material in most common use for all sorts of everyday purposes. "Long bark vessels" were used by some of the northern Algonkins in the cooking of meat and other foods,[2] most likely by means of the stone boiling method. Birch bark was a very popular raw material among these northern tribes, though it was less plentiful in the Iroquois country. One of the Relations observes of the Hurons that they were "without tables, benches, or anything of the kind, the earth or some bark serving them for every purpose."[3]

---

[1] Morgan, *League of the Iroquois*, vol. II, p. 31.
[2] *Jesuit Relations*, R. G. Thwaites ed., vol. XLI, pp. 183, 185.
[3] Ibid., vol. XXXVIII, p. 247.

The manufacture of wood into dishes, spoons, etc., was evidently a laborious process, especially before the arrival of the whites. Hennepin remarks of this that "when the Savages are about to make Wooden Dishes, Porringers or Spoons, they form the Wood to their purpose with their Stone Hatchets, make it hollow with their Coles out of the Fire and scrape them afterward with Beaver's Teeth for to polish them."[1]

Sagard also notes that the Hurons manufactured bowls from knots of wood and smoothed them with beavers' incisors.[2] The use of the latter as woodworking tools is confirmed archæologically,[3] also the employment of cutting implements of flint, bone, shell,[4] and other materials. Saws for small articles were frequently made from flint and a Grand River informant states that the rough posterior margin of the snapping-turtle's shell was used for the same purpose.

Cutting edges required to be more or less adapted in shape to the surface to which they were applied, so that tools with curved or rounded edges were soon differentiated for the making of bowls and ladles. A later adaptation and evolution of this idea is found in the curved steel knife,[5] which is found over a very large cultural area, including the eastern woodlands, and which is used everywhere for smoothing out wooden bowls and spoons. A successor of the stone gouge is a small curved adze of steel,[6] a very popular tool with woodworkers on the various reservations for roughing out such articles as bowls and falsefaces. The same implement was formerly used in the construction of dug-outs.

A favourite material for bowls everywhere was the knot which grows upon the soft maple (Plate XV). The bowls

---

[1] Hennepin, A New Discovery, p. 103.

[2] Sagard, Voyage, vol. II, p. 227.

[3] Boyle, Dr. David, Ont. Arch. Rep., 1904, pp. 20-22.

[4] Wintemberg, W. J., The Use of Shells by the Ontario Indians, Ont. Arch. Rep., 1907, pp. 42, 43. Beauchamp, N.Y. State Mus. Bulletin 41, pp. 378, 379.

[5] A Mohawk name is deyuda'sara῀tụ, cf. Oneida, diuda'sara'gda.

[6] An Oneida name by Gus Yellow, Grand River reserve, is unyonya῀da. Onondaga, djukdǫ'sää'da'. Another informant gave enakda῀sä῀nia'ta', "wooden vessels to smooth out inside."

used for playing the peach-stone game were made from the knots found on the maple, walnut, and other woods. Basswood was perhaps still more commonly employed (Plate XXV). Sassafras is mentioned by Kalm as having been used for bowls.[1] Brickell, in describing the Indians of North Carolina, states that they made "dishes and wooden platters" of the sweet gum, poplar, sycamore, and the like.[2] It is probable, that other woods were also used, according to locality and suitability for the purpose. Handles were frequently placed oppositely and were sometimes carved into various forms.

DISHES USED IN EATING.

Dishes for this purpose were made both of wood and bark, the latter, as before, showing evidences of having been the more common material and the wood, to some extent at least, the result of more modern appliances. For ordinary purposes basswood was often employed.

The convenience and utility of bark dishes and troughs is seen in their retention down to comparatively recent times, many of the older people having eaten from them and still remembering their construction. Many references are found to the use of these. Squire Johnson, in describing the customs of New York State Senecas, states that, in former times, "the dishes and spoons were also made of bark."[3] Sagard, in relating his experiences while journeying to the Huron country, states that one of his companions busied himself "in seeking two flat stones with which to crush the Indian corn upon a skin stretched out upon the ground, and afterwards to empty it into a kettle and boil it; this being cooked nicely it is placed in bark bowls, and then eaten with the aid of large wooden spoons."[4] That no time was lost in these culinary preparations is suggested by the remark that dirty stones were often used for cracking the corn.

---

[1] Kalm, *Travels*, vol. I, pp. 266, 267.
[2] Brickell, *Natural History of North Carolina*, p. 401.
[3] Caswell, H. S., *Our Life Among the Iroquois*, p. 238.
[4] Sagard, *Voyage*, vol. I, p. 45.

A couple of neatly made elm bark sap troughs were collected at Tonawanda (Plate XXIV, fig. b). In the construction of these the bark is thinned at the ends and gathered into a fan-shaped tie. The fragrant though somewhat sticky bark of young pines is frequently made into bowls by folding and tying at the ends. Basswood is also used, and Kalm records the employment of buttonwood bark.[1] The variety of these materials is suggestive in some slight degree of the ingenuity of the Iroquois in the adaptation to their needs of natural products.

Onondaga Names for Dishes Used in Eating.

Large bread bowl, ga'o'wa'.
Eating bowl, ga'o'wa' odekonia'′ta'.
Butter bowl, ewisonia'′ta' ga'o'wa'.
Bowl for peach-stone game, deyeyęda′kwa' ga′djię'
  (betting bowl).
Bark bowl, uskǫ′daa' ga'o'wa'.
Dish made of a turtle's carapace, ha'nu′wa' ga′djię'.

SPOONS OR LADLES.

Spoons were, perhaps, most frequently made of wood and are often mentioned in connexion with bark receptacles and utensils.[2] On the other hand, bark was also employed in spoon-making and spoons of this material were commonly used within the recollection of many now living on the reservations. Elm bark seems to have been most in favour and could be quickly manufactured into a serviceable article (Plate XXVI, fig. a), which was made in several styles.

Home-made spoons are occasionally used even at present (Plates XXVI, XXVII, XXVIII). Large-sized dipping spoons, sometimes nearly a foot in diameter, were formerly employed in longhouse festivities, though these have been displaced to a very large extent by tin dippers. A hook on the end of the handle

---

[1] Kalm, *Travels*, vol. I, p. 62.
[2] Loskiel, pt. I, p. 54, remarks that "they make their own spoons, and large round dishes of hardwood, with great neatness. In eating, many make use of the same spoon, but they commonly sup their victuals out of the dish."

of the dipping spoon prevents it from falling into the vessel from which soups or beverages are dispensed.

Decoctions of hemlock bark and roots, also the bark of the alder, are used in colouring spoons and other wooden articles a deep red. These become further darkened and polished by usage.

Basswood is favoured for its not warping or checking. Maple, especially the curly grained, is preferred by some. Materials noted at Onondaga Castle, New York, were apple tree root, soft maple knot, and white ash. Kalm records the use by eastern tribes of "spoon tree" (*Kalmia latifolia*); and J. D. Hunter, that of buckeye or horse-chestnut.

The handles of spoons are frequently carved with designs which are ornamental, totemistic, or in response to dreams, particularly those occurring during some indisposition or illness. The dreams are interpreted by a local seer or medical practitioner, who decides upon the design, also the kind of wood, the presentation of such dream-objects to the patient being necessitated to secure recovery. Failure in this respect is believed to be followed by continued illness and eventually by death. The custom seems to have been based upon the belief that the soul can depart from the body and that satisfaction of its desires must be obtained to bring about its return.[1]

Eating spoons vary in size, some being of quite generous dimensions. The shapes, also, are of considerable interest, some suggesting prototypes of clam-shell, others apparently being based upon spoons of horn and similar material, and others still upon the gourd-shell ladle or dipper.

Clam-shells are frequently found on Iroquois sites, suggesting a possible use as spoons, although, as remarked by W. J. Wintemberg, "We cannot be certain as to how many of the unios . . . were, if at all, used as spoons, . . owing to the fact that none of them has been altered in any way." Some of the older Iroquois, however, still carry clam-shells to eat with at festivals or ceremonies.

John Jamieson, sen., stated that clam-shells are not good to use for spoons as they cause incontinence of urine (sympathetic

---

[1] *Jesuit Relations*, R. G. Thwaites ed., vol. XLIII, p. 267.

magic—the dribbling of water from the clam when it is taken from the water suggesting the foregoing idea).

Some old-fashioned people, according to this informant, pick up all kinds of food in the fingers, using no fork nor spoon at all.

A spoon-like utensil made from the scapula of a large mammal is figured on page 27 of the Ontario Archæological Report for 1902. This was found in Brant county, a district known to have been inhabited by Iroquois. Dr. Boyle, in commenting on this specimen, remarks that: "It is seldom that anything like a spoon is found in Ontario, but occasionally there appears a specimen which would seem to have been used as such. This scarcity may be owing to the absence of spoon-food among the aborigines, or to the nature of the substance of which spoons were made—wood or thin pieces of bone, when mussel (unio) shells were not so employed." Regarding foods, however, the reverse would seem to have been the case, as soups and broths were a favourite diet. Small and rather roughly-made clay cups, which may have been also used as ladles, are occasionally found.

Small eating-paddles made of wood or hickory bark are sometimes employed even at present. The hickory bark paddles are called hesnänugaya″dę' (On.). This item was furnished by John Jamieson, jun.

David Jack has seen cow ribs sharpened to a broad edge and used in the same way as the foregoing.

Spoons and eating-sticks or forks used to be cleaned, put into a deer-skin bag, and hung up somewhere until wanted again.

Terms.

Spoon, { ado′gwat (On.).
 { ganiyu′da' (Ca.).

Bark ladle or spoon, ado′gwat oskǫ′da' (On.).

Large dipping ladle (used in longhouse), adᴜgwa·'tsɪ'wanɛ (On.).

FORKS OR EATING-STICKS.

These seem to have varied somewhat, particularly in length, being made to conform to individual preference. Some were manufactured with a hook at the handle for suspension when not in use. Models of these made by David Jack and John Jamieson, jun., were considerably over a foot in length.

At large gatherings of any kind where food is served, the chiefs and leading men often go outside, if the weather is warm, to some shady spot, where big trays of meat, corn soup, and corn bread are ready. A large basketful of pointed sticks is brought around. Each person takes one of the latter and uses it for holding his or her portion of meat or dumpling (Figure 1).

THE PADDLE.

Stirring paddles and paddles for lifting the cakes of boiled corn bread from the kettle are still quite frequently seen in Iroquois houses (Plates XXIX, XXX).

The stirring paddle is the narrower of the two and is used in the preparation of corn soup, hominy, and other foods. The bread paddles are of two styles, one having a rectangular blade, the other a blade of circular shape. The latter are stated by an Onondaga informant to have been used for turning or revolving the cakes while cooking. Most bread paddles have a circular or heart-shaped hole in the middle of the blade to assist in draining. Another use suggested for these holes is to tell when maple syrup has reached the point of "sugaring," by noting its inclination to thread across the opening.

The wood employed for paddles is usually some variety of maple, though other hardwoods are sometimes used.

The carved designs with which the handles are decorated show some variety, though no indication could be secured of any particular significance. One of the more elaborately designed paddles has at the end a wooden chain carved from the solid, from which is suspended a hollow rectangular ornament containing some wooden balls.

Terms.

Paddle.
- aserawą′yɩ' (Oneida).
- gᶒsdoᶇ gwa' (On.).
- aserawą′lyɩ' (Mo.).
- gatgo′nia'tra' (Ca.).

THE KNIFE.

This was a very necessary utensil in food preparation. Knives were of several kinds. One type, no doubt, answered for a hunting knife, for skinning and cutting up the animals killed, as well as for carving or dividing the meat after its preparation for food. The steel knife, of course, has superseded other kinds, but various materials other than steel were formerly used. One of the Relations remarks of the Iroquois that "They used a scallop or an oyster-shell for cutting off the right thumb" of a captive.[1] Clam-shells of various kinds are frequently found on Iroquoian village sites, a number showing wear and suggesting use for various purposes. Knives made from strips of elm and hickory bark are still sometimes used for skinning and fleshing and may also have been formerly employed as culinary utensils (Plate XXXI, figs. a, b).

An important cutting material throughout a very wide area was flint or chert.[2] Little is known regarding its use by the Iroquois for knives, but its suitability was hardly likely to have remained unnoted. Knife-like blades are frequently found on ancient village sites. The one illustrated was picked up on the old Iroquois reserve at Onondaga Castle, N. Y. One side of this has a rounder curve than the other and the article is evidently intended for attachment to a handle (Plate XXXI, fig. c).

FOOD MATERIALS AND RECIPES.

CORN AS A FOOD PLANT.

Corn (*Zea mays*), as a food material, was found throughout an immense area in North America, including such ethnological areas as Mexico and Central America, in the former of which

---

[1] *Jesuit Relations*, R. G. Thwaites ed., vol. XXXI, p. 45.

[2] Kalm states, probably with regard to the Iroquois and neighbouring tribes, that "they were satisfied with little sharp pieces of flint or quartz, or else some other hard kind of a stone, or with a sharp shell, or else with a piece of bone which they had sharpened."—*Travels*, vol. I, pp. 341, 342.

localities it is considered to have originated;[1] the southwestern and southeastern areas; the eastern woodlands as far north, practically, as it could be successfully cultivated; also the southern and eastern[2] borders of the plains region, where it was cultivated by Siouan, Caddoan, and other tribes. Along the Pacific coast and over the plateau area evidence is lacking that it was cultivated north of the Rio Colorado.[3]

It was found in cultivation by the early explorers of the Mississippi valley and as far northward as the Mandan and Arikara on the upper Missouri, though not along the upper Mississippi nor in more northern latitudes.

Its introduction at an early date into the regions named is indicated by its extensive distribution, its intimate association with mythology and ceremonial procedure, and by the numerous archæological remains discovered.

IROQUOIS CORN VARIETIES.

Most of the early writers who deal with ethnological topics describe the varieties of corn, though generally very loosely and inaccurately.

Hariot, in "A briefe and true report, "states that there were "some white, some red, some yellow and some blew." This makes no account of more important distinctions. He further remarks that "There are three sortes, of which two are ripe in eleven and twelve weekes at the most: . . . The other sort is ripe in fourteene, and is about ten foote high."[4]

That colour was an incomplete basis of classification was appreciated by Beverly, who distinguishes four sorts: two early

---

[1] De Candolle, *Origin of Cultivated Plants*, p. 387.

Sturtevant, *Kitchen Garden Esculents of American Origin*, Amer. Nat., vol. XIX, p. 444.

Darwin, *Varieties of Plants and Animals under Domestication*, vol. I, pp. 331, 332.

[2] Wissler, Clark, *The North American Indians of the Plains*, Pop. Sc. Monthly, May 1913, p. 438.

Gilmore, M. R., *The Aboriginal Geography of the Nebraska Country*, Reprint Proc. Miss. Valley Hist. Soc., vol. VI, pp. 6, 7.

[3] *Handbook of American Indians*, pt. I, pp. 790, 791.

[4] Hariot, *A brief and true report*, p. 24.

ripe and two late ripe. There was an early ripe ear of a "lesser size," not much larger than the handle of a case knife and with a stalk between three and four feet high. The late ripe corn was distinguished by the shape of grain only, without respect to colour, and, as he further remarks, "that therefore which makes the Distinction, is the Plumpness or Shrivelling of the Grain; the one looks as smooth, and as full as the early ripe Corn, and this they call Flint-Corn; the other has a larger Grain, and looks shrivell'd with a Dent in the Back of the Grain, as if it had never come to perfection; and this they call She-Corn. This is esteemed by the Planters, as the best for Increase."[1]

In "Discoveries and settlements of the English in America" there are mentioned such varieties as "red, white, yellow, blue, green and black, and some speckled and striped."[2]

Morgan mentions only three varieties specifically. These are: the white, "o-na-o'-ga-ant;" red, "ti'c-ne;" and the white flint, "ha-go'-wa." The latter is incorrectly referred to as Seneca bread corn.[3]

That selection was practised is shown by the number of varieties. Sagard remarks that the seed-corn used by the Hurons was "previously selected, and chosen with care."[4] The Indians also taught the New England colonists to "cull out the finest seeds," as well as to "observe fittest season."[5] Such a proceeding was doubtless quite general. It is said of the Pimas that "when gathering corn the women lay aside the best ears for seed."[6] Among the Iroquois, also, seed-corn is selected with a view to the propagation of such qualities as size, flavour, colour, and early maturity.

Dent corn has been described as a western form. The "she-corn" described by Beverly is probably a dent; also the "poketawes" of the Powhatans. J. G. Curtis, in Cyclopedia of American Agriculture, remarks that there is a "predominance of flint corns northward and of dent or pointed corns southward."

---

[1] Beverly, *History and Present State of Virginia*, vol. II, pp. 28, 29.

[2] Pinkerton, *Voyages*, vol. 12, p. 242.

[3] Morgan, *League of the Iroquois*, vol. II, p. 28.

[4] Sagard, *Voyage du Pays des Hurons*, p. 93.

[5] Wood, *New England's Prospect*, Boynton reprint, p. 74.

[6] Russell, F., *26th Annual Rep. B. A. E.*, p. 90.

The history of sweet corn is rather obscure. It was an old Indian variety, and is generally conceded to have been first introduced among the whites by Capt. Richard Begnall, an officer in Sullivan's campaign, who obtained it from the Susquehannas in 1779. It was then called "papoon corn."[1] Sturtevant in 1899 lists sixty-one sweet corn varieties, classifiable into three types.[2] The characteristic crinkled appearance of this corn is owing to its inability to develop its starch to maturity, so that, in passing from the "milky" stage to maturity, there is evaporation and wrinkling.[3]

Popcorn, also a native variety, is still used quite extensively· Botanically, it may be considered a special group of flint corn and differs from these and the dent corns but little in composition. Twenty-five varieties are recognized, which are variations of the rice or toothed and the smooth or pearl corn. These are further divisible into early, medium, and late. All the varieties cross readily, showing the same colour variations as the other types.

Podded corn, which is classed as a variety, was known from a very early date, and is a form in which each kernel is enclosed in husks or scales, usually four, in addition to the husks or foliace-

---

[1] Van der Donck, *New Netherlands* (1656). N. Y. Hist. Soc. Trans., vol. I, p. 137.

[2] Seven varieties of corn (*Zea mays*) are recognized by agriculturists viz.:
Zea mays tunicata, pod corn—probably derived from Argentina.
Zea mays everta, popcorn—possessing an excessive portion of corneous endosperm.
Zea mays indurata, flint corn—having a starchy endosperm enclosed in a corneous endosperm varying in thickness in different varieties.
Zea mays indentata, dent corn—having corneous endosperm at the sides of the kernel only, the starchy endosperm, which extends to the top of the grain, drying and thus forming the indentation.
Zea mays amylacea, soft or starchy corn—characterized by the absence of corneous material.
Zea mays saccharata, sweet corn—characterized by a translucent horny appearance and crinkling in drying. Has little or no starch.
Zea mays amylea-saccharata, starchy-sweet corn—having externally the appearance of a sweet corn, but with the lower half of the kernel starchy and non-crinkled.
J. W. Harshberger, *Cycl. of Amer. Agric.*, vol. II, p. 402.

[3] East, E. M., *A Note Concerning Inheritance in Sweet Corn.* Science, N.S., vol. XXIX.

ous bracts enclosing the ear. This has been thought by some to represent a very primitive form of maize, the naked-seeded form being a later development. The form was first described botanically by C. Bauhin in 1623, and is only morphologically, not specifically, different from the other maizes, since in all varieties the kernels possess rudimentary scales, which can be seen when the grains are removed from the ear. Podded corn, like the other varieties mentioned, can be hybridized, with a production of the usual colour variations.

All the corn varieties (Plate XXXII) are considered to be sub-divisions of the single species, *Zea mays*. Size, colour, the presence or absence of starch, the production of podded grains, and a number of other characters, all observe the laws of heredity as defined by Mendel, and may be hybridized in varying proportions or fixed to a greater or less degree by selection.[1] Variations from type are consequently of frequent occurrence.[2]

Onondaga Names for Corn Varieties—By Chief Gibson.

Zea mays amylacea (starchy or "bread" corns):
>   White corn (Tuscarora), unähagä̜'äda' "light-coloured corn" (Plate XXXII, figs. a 6, a 7).
>   Purple, unähagä̜'äda' uwę'hia', "bread corn, purple" (Plate XXXII, fig. a 2).
>   Variegated (Calico), unähagä̜'äda' deyudji'du⁻yı', "bread corn, several different colours" (Plate XXXII, figs. a 3, a 4).
>   Red, unähagä̜'äda' utgwę'daa', "bread corn, red" (Plate XXXII, fig. a 1).
>   Short white, ears covered at the ends with grains, unähagä̜'äda' deyu'niogwı'kdi', "bread corn, covered at end" (Plate XXXII, fig. a 6).
>   Light yellow (possibly a hybrid) unähagä̜'äda' udji'-tgwagä̜'äda'.

---

[1] East and Hayes, *Inheritance in Maize*, Bulletin 167, Agric. Exper. Stat., New Haven, Conn. See also bibliography, p. 138.

[2] Sturtevant, E. L., *An Observation on the Hybridization and Cross-Breeding of Plants*, Amer. Nat., vol. XIX, p. 1040.

Zea mays indurata (flint or "hominy" corns):

Flint, long ears, unäha'u̱'wɩ' deyunahasda·'tɩk deyu'-nio̱gwɩ'kdi' uwҿwe'idji's, "corn, smooth, covered at ends, long ears" (Plate XXXII, fig. b 1).

Flint, short ears, unäh'u̱'wɩ' deyunahasda·'tɩk deyu'-nio̱gwɩ'kdi', "corn, smooth, covered at ends" (Plate XXXII, fig. b 2).

Purple, short ears, unäha'u̱'wɩ' eno̱dai'ɛnia"ta', "corn, hominy".

Yellow, long ears, unäha'u̱'wɩ' udjitgwai'igo̱', "yellow corn."

Flint, variegated, covered at ends, unäha'u̱'wɩ' deyudji'-du"yɩ' eno̱dai'ɛnia"ta', "corn, several colours, for hominy" (Plate XXXII, fig. 4 b).

Zea mays saccharata (sweet corn):

Sweet corn, unäha'u̱'wɩ' undɛnäha'gei', "corn, shrunken." A short-eared "nubbin" variety was obtained at Onei-datown. This was white and covered at the ends (Plate XXXII, figs. b 6, b 7).

Zea mays everta (popcorn):

Popcorn (general name), awҿso̱"gwa' onҿ'ha', "for popping corn."

White rice popcorn, unu'djia' awҿso̱"gwa', "tooth popcorn." (Plate XXXII, fig. b 5).

Red rice, unu'djia' awҿso̱"gwa' utgwҿ"da·'dji', "tooth popcorn, dark red."

Red pearl (smooth), awҿso̱"gwa' utgwҿ"da·'dji'.

A general name given by an Onondaga Castle informant was: awҿ'so̱"gwa" u̱dä̱'su̱'kwa', "corn for popping."

An Oneida general name is: yoniso'go̱'ta'.

Zea mays amylea-saccharata (starchy-sweet):

A short-eared corn apparently belonging to this variety was obtained at Oneidatown.

Seneca Names for Corn Varieties—By Alex. Snider, Tonawanda N.Y.

Starchy or "bread" corn:
White, one'ǫgäänd.
White, grains growing over the end, he'go'wa' one'ǫ'
Yellow, djitgwä⁀ą̈ one'ǫ'.
Twelve-rowed, yellow, one'ǫ' dɩkni'skaii' nia'dɩ'.
Purple, one'ǫdji'.
Popcorn, wa'dadǫgwɑs one'ǫ'.
Black, dją̈sta⁀ą̈ wa'dakǫgwɑs one'ǫ'.

Caughnawaga (Mohawk) Names for Corn Varieties—By Mr Stacey.

Starchy or "bread" corn:
White bread corn, onąhagą'ra'.
Flint or "soup" corn;
Soup corn, yellow, onąsteu'ŋwe'.
Purple "soup," oa'nar'.
Sweet corn, degǫderu'ŋwɩks.
Popcorn, white rice, wadenąstada'gwas.

Cayuga Names for Corn Varieties—By William Harris.

Bread corn, red, utgwɑ'djia onà'hą̈.
Bread corn, variegated, na'hadji'.
Bread corn, yellow, djitgwa onà'hą̈.

Other Terms Used in Corn Culture (On.)

Ear of corn, unǫgwę⁀ya' unęhu⸱'da'.
Cornstalk, uheiɛ'.
Leaves of the corn, udjiąwa⸜sa'.
Silk, uge'eda'.
Tassel, ugwę'dà'hää'.
Cornfield, unę'ha' gaiɛ'ntwɩ'.
In the field, gahą̈dagǫ'wa'.
Hill of corn, gana'gę'shą̈'.
Corn-cob, unǫ'gwę⁀ya'.

OTHER SEEDS AND GRAINS.

The wild oat or rice (*Zizania aquatica*) appears to have been occasionally used by the Iroquois, although it was employed extensively by surrounding tribes.[1]

The sunflower (On., uwɛ'wę̨'sa') was frequently cultivated, either together with corn and beans, or in patches by itself, and[2] furnished an oil[3] which was highly esteemed. The Hurons and Iroquois generally are said to have sown but little of it, though they made from it an oil "to annoint themselves."[4] The Indians of Virginia made of it "both a kinde of bread and broth."[5].

The oil was said, by a Mohawk informant, to have been made by roasting the seeds slightly, then pounding them in a mortar, after which the material was boiled and the oil skimmed off.[6]

The oil, at present, is used principally for ceremonial purposes, such as the anointing of the masks used by the Falseface society. It was also stated by Chief Gibson to be good for the hair and to prevent it from falling out or changing colour.

Other seeds were no doubt used by the Iroquois at times. An indefinite reference in the Relations, for instance, states that the Iroquois gave to Lalement "certain seeds to eat—but so insipid and so dangerous that they served as a very quick poison to those who knew not how to prepare them."[7]

---

[1] Carr, *Foods of Certain American Indians*, Amer. Antiq. Soc. Proc., N.S., vol. X, p. 179.
Parker, *Bulletin 144, N.Y. Educ. Dept.*, p. 109.
Lafitau, *Moeurs des Sauvages, Ameriquains*, tome II, pp. 95, 96.
[2] Charlevoix, *A Voyage to North America*, vol. II, p. 91.
[3] Oil: u'na' (On.).
Sunflower oil: awaÿ'sa'u'na (Ca.).
[4] Lafitau, *Moeurs des Sauvages Ameriquains*, tome II, p. 95.
[5] Hariot, *A briefe and true report*, p. 26.
For use by Iroquois as a food, see corn recipes, also beverages.
[6] Simon Bumberry, Brant County reserve.
[7] *Jesuit Relations*, R. G. Thwaites ed., vol. XXXI, p. 91.

CORN RECIPES.[1]

The many ways employed by the Iroquois for preparing animal and vegetable foods have been frequently commented upon. There were also ways of combining these products which gave an almost unlimited variety.

Forty methods of cooking corn are frequently mentioned.[2] Dumont speaks of forty-two ways as known among the Indians of Louisiana.[3] Le Jeune refers to twenty ways observed among the Hurons.[4] There are indications, also, which suggest that recipes were derived by borrowing from surrounding nations, as were other cultural ideas.

A very large proportion of Iroquois foods were evidently of a liquid nature. This is substantiated by the numerous references to soups and broths prepared from ripe and unripe corn, beans, squashes, meats, and other materials.

These were easily prepared, were usually nourishing, and also answered the purposes of a beverage, but may have been responsible for cases of decayed teeth found.[5] Preparations of this kind are still very popular, although more variety has since been introduced.

---

[1] Information and demonstrations regarding the preparation of corn were obtained from a number of people, including Chief and Mrs. Gibson, Mr. and Mrs. Peter John, and Mrs. Simon Bumberry, Brant County reserve; Mrs. David Williams and Mrs. Tommy Day, Oneidatown. Individual items were also secured from a large number of others.

[2] Boyle, Dr. David, *Ontario Arch. Rep.*, *1898*, p. 189.

[3] Dumont, *Mémoires sur La Louisiane*, Paris, 1753, vol. I, pp. 33-34.

[4] *Jesuit Relations*, R. G. Thwaites ed., vol. X, p. 103; twelve ways, Loskiel, *Hist. of Mission*, etc., p. 67; eight ways, Champlain, *Voyages*, vol. III, pp. 162-164.

[5] The causes of decay in teeth are not definitely known. The lack of foods requiring vigorous chewing, which keeps the teeth clean naturally, is probably a factor. It has also been suggested that starchy foods, of which the Iroquois used a large amount, ferment and attack the enamel, thus forming a nidus for the germs causing decay. A marked difference between Iroquois teeth and those of tribes using fewer starchy foods and more meat has been found by Mr. F. H. S. Knowles, physical anthropologist for the Geological Survey, the amount of decay being much less among the tribes last mentioned.

Boiled Corn Bread—*gahä⁻gu⁻gwa'* (On.).

After the corn has been hulled and washed (Plates XVII and XVI), it is placed in the mortar and pounded to a meal or flour. As the pounding progresses the fine sifting basket is frequently brought into requisition (Plate XIX). The hand is used to dip the meal out of the mortar into the sifter. The large bread pan is often set on top of the mortar and the sifter shaken in both hands. The coarser particles are thrown into a second bowl or tray and are finally dumped back into the mortar to be repounded.

A hollow is next made in the flour and enough boiling water poured into it to make a stiff paste. Usage differs somewhat in this respect, cold water being used by some for mixing. The stirring paddle is often employed at first, after which the paste is kneaded with the hands. Dried huckleberries, blackberries, elderberries, strawberries, or beans may be incorporated in the mixture, beans apparently enjoying the greatest favour. The latter are previously cooked just so that they will remain whole or nearly so. Currants or raisins are sometimes used at present. Formerly the kernels of walnuts and butternuts were employed in the same way.

A lump of paste is next broken off, or about a double handful. This is tossed in the hands, which are kept moistened with cold water, until it becomes rounded in form; the surplus material forms a core at one side, usually the right, and is finally broken off. The lump is now slapped back and forth between the palms, though resting rather more on the left hand; and is at the same time given a rotary motion until a disk is formed about $1\frac{1}{2}$ to $1\frac{3}{4}$ inches thick and about 7 inches in diameter.[1] Boiling water for mixing is stated to make the cakes firmer and better to handle. No salt nor other such ingredients are used.

The loaves are immediately slid into a pot of boiling water from the paddle or from between the hands and are supported

---

[1] Informants, Mrs. Peter John and others.

Bartram, *Observations*, pp. 60, 61, in describing a repast eaten at a conference held at Onondaga Castle, N.Y., in 1743, states that the cakes of boiled bread were 6 or 7 inches in diameter and about 2 thick.

on edge by placing the paddle against them until all are in. The bread paddle, or sometimes a special circular turning paddle, is used to rotate the cakes a little when partly done, so as to cook all parts alike.

An hour is usually required for cooking, though the completion of the operation is indicated when the cakes show a tendency to float, or when the steam is given out equally all over when a cake is lifted out. The bread paddle is also employed in removing the bread from the pot. When a batch is too large for the pot, some of the cakes are boiled for five or six minutes, then removed and baked in a pan in the oven.

Boiled corn bread, while not light in the ordinary sense, is decidedly tasty when newly made. It may be sliced and eaten either hot or cold with butter, gravy, or maple syrup. An Oneidatown informant states that it is often sliced and fried in butter as we fry cornmeal or oatmeal mush.

Lafitau remarks of corn bread that "nothing is heavier or more insipid; it is a mass of flour kneaded without regard to cleanliness, without either leaven or salt. They cover it with corn leaves and cook it in the ashes or in the kettle. They often also, add oil, grease, beans and fruits. It is then still more disagreeable." He admits, however, that it is best when freshly cooked.[1]

The boiling of the corn in ashes, in bread-making, was sometimes omitted. A kettleful of water was brought to the boiling point, according to a Cayuga informant.[2] The ripe corn was added and boiled until softened a little. It was then drained in the washing basket, allowed to dry slightly, then pounded, sifted, and made into flour. This kind of flour is called ganęhana'węⁿdiꞋ (On.). A similar omission is found in the Huron process of bread-making as recorded by Sagard.[3]

Loaves of corn bread[4] were frequently carried along while travelling, though parched corn flour sweetened with maple sugar

---

[1] Lafitau, *Moeurs*, vol. II, p. 94.

[2] Mrs. Peter John.

[3] Sagard, *Voyage*, vol. I, p. 94.

[4] Champlain, *Voyages*, vol. III, p. 118, states that corn, corn bread squashes, and fish were in common use among the Hurons and that meat of other kinds was scarce.

was a more popular material. The use of corn bread for this purpose is indicated in the word "johnny-cake" from "journey-cake." The ash-cake, hoe-cake, and pone are other European adoptions.

Boiled bread, according to Chief Gibson, was frequently used as wedding bread. A girl cooked twenty cakes of corn bread with berries in them. These were taken to the house of the young man, where they were cut up and given to friends and relatives who were assembled.

Bread was sometimes made of other materials, such as beans and acorns, the latter being boiled in lye to remove the bitter taste; also of roots, such as those of the yellow pond lily and others. Loskiel remarks that the Iroquois made use of many wild herbs and roots, including parsnips, of which they made a kind of bread.[1]

It is likely that other roots, seeds, and fruits were formerly used in bread-making. A suggestion of the former use of haws in this connexion is found in the name djɪgaheˣdɪs (On.)[2] which is applied to such species as Crataegus pruinosa and Crataegus submollis.

The corn preferred for bread is almost invariably of the starchy or "bread corn" variety, which includes the white or Tuscarora, also the red, purple, and calico or variegated varieties. The flint or hominy corns are said to be sometimes employed, but are considered to be less suitable. An Onondaga informant furnishes the information that a long-eared flint corn called unäha'u̯'wɪˋ uwȩwe'idji's, makes a good, sweet bread. The corn is pounded, sifted, and winnowed without being boiled in ashes.[3]

Baked Corn Bread—ogą́hägǫ'waˋ watäˣgǫdaˣgwa' (On.).

The name signifies "under the ashes cooked," and is applied to bread baked in the embers, or on flat stones placed over the

---

[1] Loskiel, *History of Missions*, pt. I, p. 68.
[2] The name is said to signify "use for bread."
[3] Peter John.

fire. This seems to have been formerly in much favour.[1] Its disuse is probably owing to the abandonment of the open fire-place and to the general adoption of European foods.

The mixture used was practically the same as for boiled bread. About three-quarters of an hour was required for cooking. As the loaves baked somewhat more quickly on top, they were turned over to be evenly done. To tell when they were finished, the cakes were tapped with the finger. If not sufficiently cooked, they felt heavy to the touch, and when done, felt lighter and more spongy. The last part of the operation was to wash them in cold water to free them from ashes or cinders.[2]

The Senecas are said to have omitted the beans or berries. On the other hand, several informants at Grand River, Ontario, state specifically that beans, berries, and sometimes maple sugar were included in the baked corn bread mixture. Adair remarks the use of a similar food among the Choctaw and Chickasaw.[3]

Mrs. John Williams (Mo.) of Caughnawaga states that red beans used to be mixed with the paste for baked corn bread, and the whole covered with cabbage leaves or corn husks. Boiled bread is the only kind made there now.

Peter John, Grand River, Ontario, relates that some fifty or sixty years ago a fire was frequently made in the open field, while they were harvesting or husking corn, and bread baked in the ashes in the old-fashioned manner.

A single cake of this bread was said by John Echo (On.) to have formerly been placed in the coffin with a corpse.[4]

---

[1] Champlain, *Voyages*, vol. III, pp. 162-164, furnishes one of the earliest descriptions of the process.

[2] Mr. and Mrs. Peter John.

[3] Adair, *History of the American Indians*, p. 407.

[4] Besides the food which is set aside for the dead at wakes and which they are supposed to require for their own consumption, a little is sometimes put into the hand. This is to be thrown to a savage cat and dog which guard a bridge over which the dead have to pass. While the animals are devouring the food the dead person slips over in safety. Informant, Peter Atkins (Mo.) and others, Grand River, Ontario.

Other Terms Used.

Corn bread, gana'daluk (Oneida).
Washed corn bread, ganɑsto'hɑlᵕ gana'daluk (Oneida).
Hulled corn bread, gageˑho'tcʉ ohäˮgwa' (On.).
Boiled bread, yena'deros ganadarokʉ'weᵕ (Mo.).
Baked corn bread, o'gɑro'gʉ yǫdena'darʉ'ta' (Mo.).
Corn flour or meal, ote'tshä' (On.).
Indian meal (modern yellow meal), djitgwai'agǫ ote'tshä'
    (On.).
Nut meats (general term), u'nie'ɛ' (On.).

(The first term given is general. The three following are
synonymous).

Soup from Corn Bread Liquor—uhäˤgwa'gei' (On.).

Soup is often made from the liquor left after boiling corn
bread. The coarser particles left after grinding and sifting the
bread meal may be added.[1] The mixture may be sweetened
with maple sugar, or it may be seasoned with salt and butter.
The name une'sda' (On.), or une'sda' onǫ'daa', is applied to the
preparation, a term which is sometimes translated as "Indian
rice." Still another variant is made by adding sweet milk or
buttermilk and sweetening with maple or granulated sugar.
It is then called uhäˤgwa'gei' unǫ'daa' (On.). The liquor is
also drunk as a beverage along with the corn bread.[2]

Another use to which the liquor is put is in the preparation
of food for infants. The latter are said to have been sometimes
put to death by the Onondagas, when the mother died, by way
of making sure that they should not suffer from neglect. The
breast was the usual method of feeding until the child became
large enough to eat the ordinary fare, which the mother chewed
first. When the mother died, the father sometimes took corn
meal gruel in his mouth and let the baby suck it out.[3]

---

[1] A Mohawk name is wadeną̈agɛ'stǫ, or "what is left."
[2] Adair, *History*, p. 416.
[3] Sagard, *Voyages*, vol. I, p. 118.

Early Bread—ti'tganahateⁿdi^ʻ (On.).

This bread was made in the early autumn from the newly-ripened and undried corn and is considered to be valuable for invalids.[1]

The unhulled corn is placed in the mortar, a little water is added and the contents beaten to a paste. It is then moulded into loaves, which may be either boiled or baked in a pan in the oven.

Dumplings—udnhǫʻsta' (On.).

The name was translated as "rolled cake soup." In making this the corn meal is mixed with boiling water to a stiff paste, which is moulded between the hands, dipped into cold water, and made into cakes the size of ordinary dumplings. These are dropped into boiling water or boiled along with venison, the flesh of game birds, or other meats. Half an hour's cooking is required.

A fork consisting of a sharpened stick or bone was formerly used to hold the dumplings while they were being eaten (Figure 1). Such eating utensils have been used within the memory of many of the older people.

Figure 1. Eating-stick or fork for holding dumplings or meat. Actual length, about 8⅜ inches. Division of Anthropology, Museum No. III I, 918. Collected by F. W. Waugh at Grand River reservation.

Wedding Bread—e'ǫyuda'kwa' uhäⁿgwa' (On.).

Another wedding bread is made as follows: a quantity of ripe white or bread corn is taken, the finest ears being selected, shelled, pounded, and sifted, without the hulling process. Huckleberries are mixed with the meal, which is made into bread and boiled in the usual way.

Five or six cakes are sufficient, according to Chief Gibson, for a small family, though Parker mentions twenty-four.[2]

---

[1] Parker, A. C., *New York State Museum Bulletin 144*, p. 72.
[2] Parker, A. C., *New York State Museum Bulletin 144*, p. 72.

These are made by the girl's mother. The parents of the young man (plus the maternal grandmother) and those of the girl having signified their approval, the mother, or the maternal grandmother of the young woman, places the cakes in a carrying basket and, accompanied by the young woman, carries them to the door of the young man's maternal grandmother. Here, all being agreeable, the cakes are accepted, the young man's maternal grandmother notifying his mother of the proposal received. The wedding cakes are in some instances left untouched upon the doorstep, whence they are eventually removed with much humiliation.

The parents of the young man, if the suit is acceptable, next notify friends and relatives of the family to assemble, when the bread is distributed equally, and eaten. This food present is referred to as a "ratification" or an evidence that the family of the girl is agreeable to the proposal. The father or male relatives of the young man furnish meat for the festivities. Venison or bear meat was formerly preferred, though veal, lamb, or beef, etc., are now in use. The young man's mother fills the empty basket which contained the wedding cakes and returns it to the girl's relatives, saying, "This is our ratification." The latter in their turn have a family meeting, at which the present of meat and other articles is consumed.

A meeting of the two families is afterward called, at which the chiefs or other leading men make speeches, give good advice to the newly married couple, and express their pleasure at seeing these families united. Old customs, however, in this respect, have been so largely discontinued that the complete marriage ceremony is seldom carried out at present.

A variant of wedding bread was made like ordinary boiled bread; but, instead of being made into rounded cakes or loaves, it was divided into smaller portions, which were formed into double packages by tying them in corn-husks. Peter John and wife stated that corn leaves were frequently used for this (Plate XXXIII, fig. c).

A variation of this recipe was given by Chief Gibson, who stated that a quantity of hulled corn meal is prepared. Pumpkin is sliced, boiled to a thin mush, and mixed with the meal and berries. The double packages are made in the following manner: some dried corn husks are taken and a number tied together at one end with basswood bark; some of the paste is filled into the husks, which are finally tied at the other end and again in the middle, forming a package somewhat like a small dumbbell. These are boiled for an hour and are usually eaten with butter.

The use of this form of corn bread at quite an ancient date among the Iroquois is indicated by Sagard, who describes it as "the bread made like two balls joined together." The Huron name was "coinkia."[1]

There seems to have been formerly a definite connexion between the double wedding bread package and the idea of marriage. Peter John described it as indicating that there was "enough bread for two together." There may have been an idea that the double package would act as a charm to hold the two together. Another item regarding the significance of wedding bread packages was furnished by a Seneca residing at Tonawanda, N.Y., who stated that formerly, when a marriage occurred at a suitable season, the present made by the young man's relatives to those of the young woman sometimes consisted of green corn, done up in a single corn-leaf package of rounded form (Plate XXXIII, fig. a). This bread was called in Seneca, deganǫh꜌stia'gǫ ä꜌gwa' (panis uno testiculo similis).

Corn and Pumpkin Bread—dega꜌niǫsayı꜌sdiꜜ uhä꜌gwa' (On.).

Corn and pumpkin were frequently combined in the preparation of foods. For bread-making, the corn is hulled and pounded into meal. A quantity of the pumpkin is sliced and boiled to a thin mush. It is then mixed with the cornmeal, to which blackberries or huckleberries have also been added. Basswood leaves are placed on the bottom and sides of a pan, into which the paste is then emptied, covered with more basswood leaves, and placed in the oven to bake. The name signifies "pumpkin mixed."

---

[1] Sagard, *Voyage*, vol. I, p. 94.

Corn and Pumpkin Pudding—udji'sgwa' or dega'ni'ǫsayı'sdi'-udji'sgwa'. (On.).

The pumpkin is boiled, as before, to a thin mush. A quantity of ripe corn is parched, pounded in the mortar, and sifted to a fine meal. The latter is then stirred into the pumpkin with a paddle, until it is of the proper thickness. Maple sugar is added to sweeten, also a little lard. The mass thickens up like a pudding, after which it is ready for eating.

Parched Corn Travelling Food—uninhǫ"da' (On.).

There was apparently no more popular travelling or hunting food than this preparation in olden times. It was light, nourishing, and could be eaten either cooked or raw. It is rarely used at present, except on certain ceremonial occasions, such as False-Face Society functions.

In making it, the white Tuscarora and other kinds of bread corn are employed. The ripe corn is shelled, parched slightly in the embers, as for popping, thrown into the mortar, some maple sugar added, and the whole pounded and sifted together to a rather fine meal. When intended for pudding or soups, rather than for eating raw, the maple sugar may be left out. Dried fruit, such as cherries, is said to have been pulverized with it at times.

Sugar is not used when the food is intended for hunters or for athletes, as it would make them dizzy (the sugar being derived from the maple, the branches of which sway about in the wind). The uninhǫ"da' is also at times mixed up with chopped meat.

It was prepared for use in several ways. It might be eaten raw in small quantities, though more than a small handful was considered dangerous without cooking, on account of its tendency to swell. On hunting expeditions or in time of war a small wooden cup or bowl was carried along. A little water was taken in this and a small amount of the meal added.[1] When game was found or when the enemy was vanquished, it was added to the

---

[1] See Beverages; informant, Thomas Key, Brant County reserve.

venison or other provisions secured. Bartram notes of this food that "about one-quarter of a pound, diluted in a pint of water, is a hearty travelling dinner."[1]

Historical references to the food are numerous, showing conclusively its common use throughout the Iroquois and Algonkin region.[2] Champlain states that very dry Indian corn was used in its manufacture. It was roasted in ashes, brayed to a meal and, in preparing it for food, they cooked a large quantity of fish and meat, cut it into pieces, skimmed off the fat, and added the meal of roasted corn, cooking the whole to a thick soup. This was among the Huron and eastern Algonkins.[3] Beverly also furnishes some information: The Indians of Virginia frequently took with them on their journeys "a Pint or Quart of Rockahomonie, that is, the finest Indian corn, parched and beaten to a powder. When they find their stomachs empty (and cannot stay the tedious Cookery of other things) they put about a spoonful of this into their Mouths, and drink a Draught of Water upon it, which stays in their stomachs."[4]

A Tonawanda informant described its use by Seneca athletes in running. A decoction should also be prepared of the toad rush, *Juncus bufonius*, the fact of its growing beside the runner's pathway being considered significant. A handful of the plant is steeped in nearly a pailful of water. The idea is to provoke vomiting. The person using it must drink about two quarts the first time, vomit, drink the same quantity, and vomit again. The face and body are also washed with the liquid. This is done about three times during the week before the race. Only sweet milk and Indian corn bread, ągweⁿąwı' äⁿgwa' (Sen.), are to be eaten. A quantity of the scorched cornmeal is carried along to eat while running, a little being taken now and again. The Seneca name for the meal is wadęⁿsondɑk one'ǫ, or "burnt

[1] Bartram, *Observations*, p. 71.
[2] Sagard, *Voyage*, vol. I, p. 142; also p. 95.
  Jesuit Relations, R. G. Thwaites ed., vol. XXIII, p. 187.
  Van der Donck, *N. Y. Hist. Soc. Coll.*, series 2, vol. I, pp. 193, 194.
[3] Champlain, *Voyages*, vol. III, pp. 162-164.
[4] Beverly, *Hist. of Virginia*, p. 155.

corn." Mrs. John Williams of Caughnawaga gave wanǫhǫ'sǫ o'nǫsdɛ' as a Mohawk equivalent.

Hulled Corn Soup—unɛha'seⁿ unähuⁿgwa' (On.).

The name for this may be translated as "corn not quite ripe yet soup." This is a favourite dish with the Iroquois both at the longhouse and at social gatherings. The corn is taken when it has become quite firm, but not yet perfectly ripe; it is then boiled with ashes, hulled and washed, boiled for half an hour and washed again, much the same as for corn bread.

Next, according to one popular recipe, it is placed along with meat, game, or with green beans in the pod, boiled slowly for about two hours, then seasoned to taste. Mrs. John Williams of Caughnawaga mentioned the use of hulled corn boiled with beans and meat. A Mohawk name for this is onǫ'sdo.

By another method, the hulled corn, after being duly prepared, is thrown into the mortar along with a little water and crushed slightly. It is then placed in a pot or kettle, some water added, also berries and a little sugar, after which it is boiled until done. With the berries added it is called unɛha'seⁿ wahi-yuⁿwi' (On.), and in any case makes a very palatable dish. It is frequently used at festivals, such as the Big Green Corn Dance.

Corn Soup with Nut Meats—u'nie·'ɛ' u'ne·ga·'geι' (On.).

Nut meats of various kinds may be added to corn soup Beechnuts were given by a Tonawanda informant[1] as a popular ingredient there, also dried apples.

The kernels are pounded in the mortar, sifted, and added to the soup, which is stirred from time to time and seasoned with salt and pepper.

Corn Soup with Sunflower Seeds—uɛ'wɛⁿsa' u'ne·ga·'geι' (On.).

Sunflower seeds are pounded and sifted to a fine meal. Soup of ripe corn and beans is prepared in the usual way. The sunflower meal is added, forming a very rich soup. This is also seasoned according to taste.

---

[1] Barber Black.

Hominy—unǫ'daa' (*On.*).

Probably no corn or other food is referred to so frequently as hominy, or sagamité, as it was more familiarly known to the early French. It was extremely simple of preparation, very often being little more than cornmeal and water. A reference in the Relations to Huron customs remarks that "the best food usually eaten there is only a paste made with meal of Indian corn boiled in water."[1]

The Relation of 1640 states: "Our entire nourishment consists of a sort of soup made of Indian corn, crushed between two stones, or pounded in a mortar, and seasoned with smoked fish,—this served in a large wooden dish."[2] A reference to an ancient Seneca form of sagamité speaks of "Indian corn and beans cooked in clear water, without seasoning."[3] The Relation of 1638-39 notes that "Sometimes the savages put in pieces of cinders to season the sagamité, at other times a handful of little water-flies, which are like the gnats of Provence. . . The more prudent keep some fish after the fishing season, to break into the sagamité during the year; . . . the more tainted the fish is the better.[4] As for drinks, they do not know what these are,—the sagamité serving as meat and drink."[5] Loskiel also calls it one of the most common of Iroquois foods.

Sagard, after describing the Huron dish called eschionque, or sagamité, made of parched corn flour, informs us that "for ordinary sagamité, which they call ottet, raw corn is used, made into flour, without separating the latter from the coarser portion, which they cook plain, with a little meat or fish, if they have such, and also mixing at times squashes cut into pieces, if it should be their season, and often enough nothing at all; for fear that the meal may stick to the pot, they stir it frequently with the estoqua, then eat it."[6] Oil is also mentioned in another Relation as a favourite ingredient of "sagamita."[7]

---

[1] *Jesuit Relations*, R. G. Thwaites ed., vol. XXXV, p. 153 (1649-50).

[2] Ibid., vol. XVIII, p. 11.

[3] Ibid., vol. XLII, p. 71.

[4] Champlain, *Voyages*, vol. III, pp. 162-164, mentions a food of this character in which tainted fish was used.

[5] *Jesuit Relations*, R. G. Thwaites ed., vol. XV, p. 163.

[6] Sagard, *Voyage*, vol. I, p. 95.

[7] *Jesuit Relations*, vol. V, p. 286.

Roger Williams applies the name of nasaˈump (samp) to "a kind of Meale Pottage, unpartch'd." He further remarks that "the English samp is corn, beaten and boiled and eaten hot or cold with milk or butter." This was among the "Nariganset" and neighbouring tribes.[1]

Hominy, properly speaking, is prepared from the flint corn. The ordinary procedure is to place a suitable quantity of the shelled grain into the mortar. A little water is added, say a ladleful or three or four tablespoonfuls, sometimes also a very small quantity of soda. The corn is pounded slowly at first, in order to loosen the hulls, then more vigorously, until it is broken up into coarse particles. It is then sifted, the coarser replaced in the mortar, and the pounding continued. The portion left after the second sifting is thrown away. The meal is next winnowed by tossing in a bowl or basket, the latter receptacle being held so as to expose the contents as much as possible to the wind. The coarser hulls are frequently brushed away with the wing of a fowl.[2] A bark fan is referred to by Sagard,[3] who also mentions the "plat à vanner," or flat vessel used for winnowing.[4] Loskiel apparently refers to this procedure in one of his "twelve ways of dressing corn," where he mentions that "they grind it as fine as flour by means of a wooden pestle and mortar, clear it from the husk and make a thick pottage of it."[5]

Unqˈdaaʼ, or corn soup, may also be made from other kinds of corn, such as popcorn, which is really a flint, and from bread corn, hulled in the ordinary way and ground to a meal. An Oneidatown informant[6] stated that the name onondaˣ is applied there to hulled and crushed corn mush cooked without meat, also to a soup prepared with meat. Beans may also be used. The latter are cooked separately so as to keep them whole, and at the proper time they are added to the corn soup. Pork,

[1] Williams, Roger, *Key*, p. 33.
[2] Informant, Peter John (On.).
[3] Sagard, *Voyage*, vol. I, p. 95.
[4] See also Smith's *Virginia* in Pinkerton's *Voyages*, vol. 13, p. 32.
[5] Loskiel, *History*, p. 67.
[6] Henry Danford.

beef, chicken, etc., are often used as a basis. Another informant[1] from the same locality stated that a mush of hulled corn,
pounded to quite a fine meal, is made and eaten with or without
milk and sugar, in the same way as rice or porridge. Still
another Oneidatown recipe refers to the use of salmon—dodiaᴿ ᴅᴜ.
The fish was hung up in the sun until rotten. A pointed stick
was stuck into the abdomen, letting the rotted flesh and other
contents run into a dish or pot of onondaᴿ. These were cooked
together and were considered delicious.

At the Oneidatown Bear Dance, the foods used are cracked
corn soup with beans and sugar, also a green corn dish called
ho'lä·. Hominy, in the shape of soup or mush, is used at other
ceremonial festivities, including the Strawberry Dance. A
Seneca name applied to this dish is onondä·ä'. The same
name is sometimes used for a green corn soup, or to a soup made
of the whole grain hulled by boiling in ashes.

Coarse Hominy—onɩsdu'wanɛ's (On.).

Soup made from a coarse hominy meal is frequently called
onɩsdu'wanɛ's, a word signifying "coarse particles." Sunflower
oil or butter may be added.

Dried Pumpkin Hominy—una'u'ŋgaa' unǫ'daa' (On.).

Another variant of hominy is made by boiling the coarse
meal (onɩsdu'wanɛ's) to a thin mush. Dried pumpkin is previously put into water, pounded slightly, sifted in the coarse
hominy basket, and added to the boiling hominy. It should
boil for about two hours. It is eaten with milk and sugar.
The name means "dried pumpkin hominy."

Early Hominy—deganɛhi'a'gi· unǫ'daa' (On.).

This is a favourite dish about the time the flint or hominy
corn has ripened, but has not yet been dried. The grain is
shelled, placed in the mortar, pounded lightly so as to crush it a
little, then thrown into boiling water. Whole beans not quite

---

[1] Anthony Day.

ripe are added; the boiling is continued until the hominy is cooked. It is then seasoned to suit with butter and salt.

A second way is to put in milk or cream and sugar instead of other seasoning materials. This makes a sweet soup.

Another way is to slightly crush a suitable quantity of the corn and beans and boil these with beef, venison, or any kind of game. Salt and pepper are used for seasoning.

Early Corn Pudding—*utcu*ʻ*gwana'wę*ʻ *udji'sgwa'* (*On.*).

The first step in preparing early corn pudding is the same as for early bread, except that the corn is pounded to a rather moist meal which is rather hard to sift.

Some pork is first boiled and the meal stirred into it with a paddle, so as to make, when it begins to swell, a thick pudding. The name was translated as "soft corn pudding."

Popcorn Mush or Pudding—*awę*ʻ*sǫⁿgwa'* *udji'sgwa'* (*On.*).

Popcorn, awęʻsǫⁿgwa', is the basis of a number of dishes which are highly in favour. It is very commonly popped and eaten and is considered a great dainty, as well as a treat for visitors. It was formerly popped by throwing it on the hot coals in an open fire-place, stirring it quickly, then pulling it out as it popped.

For popcorn pudding, the corn is first popped, then pounded and sifted, and last of all boiled by adding to hot water until it thickens to the consistency required. This is eaten with syrup, sugar, and milk or cream, also with sour milk.

Popcorn Soup or Hominy.

The meal is prepared in the same way as for the mush or pudding, but was described as being more like hominy, particularly the kind called onısdu'wane's.

The soup can be prepared in two ways: first, by boiling the meal along with some such meat as venison or beef, adding salt to season. This kind is called u'ne'gaⁿget' (On.). A second method is to make a sweet soup by adding maple sugar. This is cooled and eaten with milk. The Onondaga name given was uwɛnowę'daⁿget'.

Green Corn on the Cob—gano̦ꞌgwȩⁿyu̧ꞌ (*On.*).

A simple and always popular method of cooking green corn is to pluck it when the kernels have become somewhat firm, but are still milky. Bread corn is very commonly used in this way, though the sweet corn, *Zea mays saccharata*, is considered best.

The ears are left enveloped in the husks, placed in boiling water, and cooked for half an hour or so, or until considered done. This was formerly eaten without seasoning of any sort, though butter is often used at present.[1]

A process of parching or roasting is often applied to boiled corn left over from a meal, although batches are often boiled, roasted slightly, then shelled and dried for winter use. This way of preparing corn is referred to by early writers.

The boiled green corn may also be removed from the cob and dried without parching. This is one of the simplest methods of preservation, and is frequently mentioned historically. Corn preserved in this way may be either cooked as a soup or "sagamité", or along with venison and other meats. An Oneida name given for a soup of this kind was ho'lä·.

Succotash—ugo̦ⁿsää̀ꞌ uno̦ꞌdaaꞌ (*On.*).

This food, like a number of the others mentioned, was used throughout a very wide area in America, confirming the suggestion that food recipes were often exchanged.

Carver speaks of succotash as being in use among the "Ottagaumies, Saukies" and neighbouring nations. This consisted of "unripe corn and beans in the same state, boiled with bears' flesh."[2] The "Akansea" and other tribes of the southern plains region were found using similar recipes. Sagamité made of green corn is mentioned in the same connexion, also green corn seasoned with the peach and the squash.[3]

---

[1] Charlevoix, *A Voyage to North America*, vol. II, p. 93.
[2] Carver, J., *Travels*, p. 263.
[3] *Jesuit Relations*, R. G. Thwaites ed., vol. LXV, p. 117.

Roger Williams refers to "boiled corn whole," which was called by the "Nariganset" msi´ckquatash.[1]

A Seneca method of making this dish is to scrape off the green corn with a knife, pound the corn before cooking, then dip out of the mortar with a ladle the juice which has been squeezed out in the pounding process and add it to the boiling soup. The name given was onondä´ä', which is the general name for soup.[2]

Various kinds of vegetables in their season, such as beans, peas, pumpkins, were boiled with the corn. Mrs. John Gibson gave two methods for making succotash or green corn soup. The first was to cut the corn from the cob with a knife, or with the half of a deer's jaw with the articular portion or ramus broken off (Plate VI, fig. c). This is called, in Onondaga, egǫsigä´ia'ta'. The corn is then placed in a kettle, some boiling water added, also a quantity of whole beans which are not quite ripe. Salt and butter are added to suit the taste. A second way differed in the seasoning, which was sugar, that of the maple being preferred when convenient. A name received at Caughnawaga for green corn was o´hǫdɛ' niganǫsto´dǫ (the corn is green). A name for green corn soup was oga'sero´da' onǫdara'. The first word in the latter expression was said to be an old word for green corn.[3]

Parched Green Corn Soup—unähuⁿgwa' wadi'djiä´hä' (On.).

Green corn, when nearly ripe, is gathered, roasted on the cob before the fire, or on the top of the stove, then shelled, dried over the stove, or in the sun, in an evaporating basket (Plate XXXV, figs. a, b), then put away in a bag or barrel for future use. Grain prepared in this manner is called wadi'djiä´hä' ganähugä´yǫ (On.), or "dried parched corn."

To cook, place a quantity of the corn in a kettle, add boiling water and boil for half an hour, drain, add fresh water, then some kind of meat. Boil for an hour and season with salt. Another way of seasoning is to sweeten.

[1] Williams, Roger, *Key into the Language of America*, p. 33.
[2] Alex. Snider, Tonawanda, N.Y.
[3] Mrs. John Williams (Mo.).

Sagard gives some interesting particulars regarding utensils and methods among the Hurons: "The neintahouy is made as follows: the women roast a quantity of the corn ears, before they are quite ripe, leaning them against a stick resting on two stones before the fire, and turning them around from time to time until they are roasted sufficiently, or to do it more expeditiously they place the ears in a heap of sand which has first been heated to a high temperature by means of a fire which has been built on top of it, they then detach the grains, dry them in the sun, spread them out upon pieces of bark, after which they are stored in a receptacle (tonneau) with a third or a quarter portion of beans, agaressa, which they mingle with it, and when they wish to eat of it they boil it whole in their pot or cauldron,.. with a little fish, fresh or dry, if they have it on hand."[1]

Green Corn Soup—unɛha'se" unähu"gwa' (On.).

Green corn is husked and shelled from the cob with the hands. A fire is made outside. When a good bed of coals has been obtained, the embers are packed down level, the corn thrown on top and stirred with a stick, the coals being pulled over the corn a little. When the latter is sufficiently cooked, the ashes and fire are pulled away, the corn put into a coarse hominy basket, and the ashes and coals sifted out, after which it is washed with cold water, and boiled in a kettle with meat and beans. Salt is added, also pepper, if desired, although the latter is not much used.[2]

Green Corn Baked—ogǫ'sää' uhä"gwa' (On.).

A way of preparing green corn[3] that is much enjoyed is to scrape the green corn off with the deer's jaw scraper, place it in a pan, and bake it into a cake, somewhat of the consistency of corn bread. This is said to be excellent with hot bread and butter.

This dish has been thought to be of comparatively modern invention, although it could have been quite readily baked in

---

[1] Sagard, *Voyage*, vol. I, p. 95.
[2] Pinkerton's *Voyages*, vol. 12, p. 258.
[3] Mrs. Lyons, Onondaga Castle, and others.

earthenware vessels, on flat stones, or in the embers. Morgan makes mention of it in 1850. The name signifies "green corn bread or cake."

Dried Corn Soup—ogǫ'sää' udji'sgwa' (On.).

When not required for immediate use, the baked corn just described is broken up into small pieces, dried in the sun or over the stove and stored away for future reference. This makes an excellent soup, or "pudding," when soaked a little, then boiled and seasoned.

Roasted Corn in the Ear—wadɛ'djiä'hä' unǫ'gwɛⁿya' (On.).

One of the commonest methods of preparing green corn is to roast it before the fire and eat it without further preparation, though butter and salt are often used at present.

Champlain states that "corn freshly roasted is highly esteemed."[1] Many other observers describe the same method of preparation. A slight variation practised was to roast the ears in hot ashes.

A method in vogue, particularly some years ago, was to dig a trench in the ground, build a good fire in it so as to get a good bed of embers, then place a stout stick lengthwise over the top with the ends resting on a couple of stones. The ears of green corn were then leaned against the stick on both sides and turned from time to time until they were roasted. The corn was then eaten with or without salt and butter. It may also be scraped off and dried for future use.

A Seneca name given for roasted corn in the ear was wade''-djeàụdɑk. To roast corn is ǫde'dje'ạudę'. A Caughnawaga name is yɑdenɑ gwɑ'ɑta' oga'sero'da'.

Young people, according to S. Anderson (Mo.), are told that if they break a cob of green corn into pieces instead of eating it from the whole cob, they will be chased by o'na''tsa', a malevolent being which is believed to consist of legs only. This

---

[1] Champlain, *Voyages*, p. 163.

creature is said to frequent lonely places in the forest and always indicates by his appearance some misfortune, such as a death in the family.

Green Corn Leaf Bread—uniá'tsha' (On.).

According to Chief Gibson, the leaves are sometimes folded on the midrib, then doubled over at each end to form an oblong envelope or pocket some 4 or 5 inches long. This is filled with green corn scraped from the cob with a knife or the deer's jaw scraper. Another envelope a little longer is slipped over the first so as to make a closed package, which is tied once around the middle with basswood bark. The corn is frequently pounded to a paste in the mortar before using, though this is considered unnecessary when the scraper is employed. The packages are cooked for about three-quarters of an hour.

Another method of making into packages was given by a Tonawanda Seneca.[1] This consisted of filling a small quantity of the paste into a corn leaf bent double, then covering it around in the same way with other leaves, a sufficient number being used to prevent the contents from escaping. A string of bark is then wrapped several times around the leaves just above the ball of paste and tied. Cooked and shelled green beans are often added to the paste. Berries are used for the same purpose; also apples cut up small; or meat, such as that of the deer.

A Cayuga name given by David Jack for the smaller club-shaped packages, tied at one end, was u^{tn}hǫ'sta' (similis testiculo). The longer packages of a similar shape are called gania'-tsha', which means a "bob" or bunch of hair, similar to that worn by the women. A large cake-like leaf-package is called una''daa' gadjǫwa'sǫ (bread wrapped in corn leaves). All these forms are frequently used at the Green Corn Dance, as well as for home consumption. The smaller packages were often cooked in the broth made in cooking venison. The packages are sometimes broken open and the contents dried. All of those described are exactly similar to those used in the making of leaf and wedding bread.

---

[1] Alex. Snider.

When the corn is done, the coverings are removed and the contents eaten with butter, salt, etc. Formerly sunflower oil or bear's grease was used in place of the latter.

Historical references to leaf bread among the Iroquois and surrounding nations are numerous. Adair refers to a similar preparation in use among the Chickasaw and neighbouring tribes, which was made of chestnuts and corn. Both were taken when green and full-grown. The chestnut kernels were half boiled, the green corn was sliced from the ear and both were pounded in the mortar, then kneaded, wrapped in corn blades to form packages about an inch thick, and boiled. A sort of boiled bread was mentioned, which was mixed with beans and potatoes.[1]

Sagard describes a leaf-bread made by the ancient Hurons, which he found little to his liking. The "women, girls and children with their teeth detach the grains which they eject into large bowls which they have at hand, and finish by pounding it in the large mortars; and as this paste is very syrupy it is of necessity wrapped in the leaves to cook it under the ashes according to the custom. This chewed bread is the most highly esteemed among them."[2]

OBSOLETE CORN FOODS.

The earlier historical accounts describe a number of Iroquois foods, the use of which has been discontinued.

Green corn on the cob, for example, is probably seldom eaten raw at present, though Lafitau remarks that "when the Indian corn is yet soft and almost milky, it is crushed slightly without separating it from the cob; it is then very agreeable to the taste."[3] This seems to have been most frequently used in emergencies, or when lack of time prohibited further preparation. The use is noted among the New York Iroquois of "very short rations consisting solely of Indian corn just picked." This was in the Relation of 1652-53.

---

[1] Adair, *History of the American Indians*, pp. 407, 408.
[2] Sagard, *Voyages*, vol. I, p. 94.
[3] Lafitau, *Moeurs*, vol. II, p. 93.
Jesuit Relations, R. G. Thwaites ed., vol. XL, p. 151.

Cornstalks were sometimes utilized, according to Bartram,[1] who observed some of the Iroquois "chewing raw Indian cornstalks, spitting out the substance after they sucked out the juice." These are said to have been found quite sweet and palatable by many. Smith's "Virginia" mentions the same food, also such recent writers as Mrs. H. S. Caswell in "Our Life Among the Iroquois." A number of the older people still remember seeing sections of cornstalk cut between joints and chewed as a means of quenching thirst.

The use of stinking corn by the Hurons is described quite graphically by Sagard: "For leindohy, or bled puant, a large quantity of ears is taken, not yet perfectly ripe and dry, so as to be more susceptible to the acquisition of the odor, and this the women place in some pond or puddle of stagnant water, for a period of two or three months, at the end of which they remove it and this serves as a material for feasts of much importance, cooked as neintahouy, and they also eat it roasted under the hot cinders, licking their fingers while handling these stinking ears, as though they were bits of sugar cane, notwithstanding that the taste and odor are vile, and more infectious than the filthiest gutters."[2] Champlain also refers to the "corn rendered putrid in pools or puddles." No recollection of this dish was found among present-day Iroquois.

A quotation is given by Parker to the effect that "when they were travelling or lying in wait for their enemies they took with them a kind of bread made of Indian corn and tobacco juice, which, says Campanius, was a very good thing to allay hunger and quench thirst in case they have nothing else at hand."[3]

CEREMONIAL CORN FOODS.

Bear's Pudding—u'gwai'i'nehaⁿ (On.).

This was described by Chief Gibson as consisting of corn soup or hominy made in the usual way, but seasoned with sugar.

---

[1] Bartram, *Observations*, p. 47.
  Pinkerton's *Voyages*, vol. 13, p. 32.
[2] Sagard, *Voyage*, vol. I, p. 97.
  Champlain, *Voyages*, vol. III, p. 162.
[3] Vincent, *History of Delaware*, Phila., 1870, pp. 74, 75.

Meat was said not to be used in that locality at all, the idea being to prepare foods which a bear is supposed to like.

The services of the Bear Society may be indicated by a dream or by some other circumstance which may be interpreted by the local "fortune-teller" to mean that a meeting of the society is required as a medical procedure.

The person requiring the ceremony must prepare the corn soup, also some sweetened juice or wine of huckleberries or blackberries. When the society meets, tobacco is burned and speeches are made asking the bear to relieve the patient. The leader then takes a drink of the blackberry juice, and also gives a little to the patient. They then sing to the accompaniment of horn rattles and the water drum. The leader begins the dancing, the others falling in. If the sick person can dance, it is so much the better. At the end of the ceremony there is a distribution of the soup.

Buffalo Dance Pudding—*deyuna*ᵛgai'änta' (On.).

The buffalo dance pudding is used by members of the Buffalo Society or Company. A meal is made of bread corn and is used in the preparation of a thick pudding sweetened with maple or other sugar. It is intended to represent the mud in which the buffalo wallows. The necessity for the ceremony is indicated in a similar manner to that for the Bear Dance ceremony. An Oneidatown recipe includes the addition of beef to the pudding.

Ball Players' Pudding—*gadji*ᵏgwae'' (On.).

When a person has been suffering from some ailment such as rheumatism, lame back, fever, or headache, it may be decided, as before, that a game of lacrosse is required. The leader of the players is notified. The sick person then prepares a quantity of white bread or Tuscarora corn. This is parched or roasted, pounded, and sifted to a fine meal. A large potful of water is brought to a boil, the meal stirred in, and some maple or other sugar added, also some fried pork and gravy, the whole being boiled to form a mush.

There is usually to be found in such ceremonies some connexion, imaginary or otherwise, between the illness and the remedy proposed, the ball game possibly suggesting that the activity of the players will remove any sickness affecting the activity of the patient. At the end of the game the mush or pudding is consumed by those present.

False-face Pudding—gagǫⁿsa' hodidji'sgwa' (On.).

The False-face pudding is eaten both at the regular meetings of the False-face Society, as well as when the services of the Society are invoked in certain ailments. The pudding is also made of parched corn meal and maple sugar boiled to form a "mush" or pudding, sunflower or bear's oil being sometimes used as a seasoning.

The food is supposed to be specially pleasing to the False-faces, who have the power of distorting the faces of those who speak disrespectfully while participating in the ceremony and particularly while eating the pudding.[1] The patient must eat along with the others.

BEANS AND BEAN FOODS.

Beans of various kinds appear to have been connected from an early date with Iroquois agriculture, and, like corn and certain other products, to have become interwoven with a number of mythological concepts. The "Three Sisters," aⁿsę nadegǫdä'nǫ'dää' (On.), for instance, were a well-known trinity of deities, the guardian spirits of corn, beans, and squashes. The bean is also associated more or less intimately with the annual ceremonies of planting-time and thanksgiving after harvest.

The beans cultivated are mostly of the genus *Phaseolus*, which is considered to have been indigenous to South America. The genus includes, also, the Limas and the runners [2] (Plate XXXIV).

---

[1] Parker, A. C., *New York State Museum Bulletin 144*, p. 79.

[2] Common, or kidney bean, *Phaseolus vulgaris*; Lima bean, *Phaseolus lunatus;* Runners (Scarlet, etc.), *Phaseolus multiflorus.*

The Jesuit Relations and the accounts of most early writers abound in references to bean culture and to the many varieties which were met with among the Iroquois and other tribes. Beverly, in describing the agriculture of the Virginia Indians, among whom were no doubt included the Cherokee, remarks that "they likewise plant a Bean in the Same Hill with the Corn, upon whose stalk it sustains itself. The Indians sow'd Peas (beans, evidently) sometimes in the Intervals of the Rows of Corn, but more generally in a Patch of Ground by themselves. They have an unknown Variety of them, but all of a Kidney-Shape, some of which I have met with wild."[1] Cartier noted that the Indians met with on his voyages had "beans of all colors, yet differing from ours."[2] Josselyn mentions beans which were "white, black, red, yellow, blue, spotted, besides your Bonivis and Calavances, and the kidney-bean that is proper to Roanoke. But these are brought into the country; the others are natural to the climate."[3] Pole or climbing beans were evidently planted with the corn and the dwarf varieties by themselves.

Over sixty different bean varieties were collected by the writer; of these some fifty or more were cultivated by Professor R. B. Thomson and H. B. Sifton of the University of Toronto, to whom the writer is indebted for a number of the identifications given.

Horticultural varieties have been included, as the history of these is so obscure, in many cases, as to suggest that they may have been more or less directly due to Indian horticulture.[4]

Beans of all kinds are roughly classified by the Iroquois into "bread beans" and "soup beans," the former being used in the making of corn bread, and the latter as an ingredient of soup. The classification naturally varies with individual preference. Beans of a short, round type are further referred to as "cranberry."

---

[1] Beverly, *History and Present State of Virginia*, vol. II, p. 29.
[2] Cartier, *Bref Récit*, p. 31.
[3] Josselyn, *Voyages*, pp. 73, 74.
[4] Jarvis, C. D., *American Varieties of Beans*, Cornell University Bulletin, No. 260.

The following are some of the more frequently occurring kinds:

Cranberry Beans.[1]

1. White with maroon and buff markings ventrally or around the eye; identified as Golden Wax (Plate XXXIV, fig. f 2):
   niyuę'sagwahaha⋏yuk deyuditgwę'daąda' (On.):
   gahutsheragą'ra osahe'ida' (Mo.).

2. White; resembles White Marrow or Cranberry (Plate XXXIV, fig. a 1):
   na⋏yuk (Ca.); α⋏yuk u'sahei'dagä'äda (On.).

3. Maroon; pole, poor climber; resembles Arlington Red Cranberry; collected at Oneidatown, Ontario (Plate XXXIV, fig. a 2).

4. Black; climbing (Plate XXXIV, fig. a 3):
   α⋏yuk niyuę'sagwaha (On.).

5. Light buff with brownish ring around hilum or eye; climbing (Plate XXXIV, fig. a 4):
   α⋏yuk uę'sis eha'ta' u'gwę'da' (On.).

6. Light yellow or sulphur-coloured; identified as Eureka (Plate XXXIV, fig. a 5):
   α⋏yuk dji'twga' (On.).

7. Buff, splashed and speckled with maroon (Plate XXXIV, fig. a 6):
   ga'huŋk udisahe'i'da' (On.), or Wild Goose Bean;
   ha⋏yuk (Ca.), applied to a similar bean.

Bread Beans.

8. Buff with maroon stripes and markings; a large-sized bean; bush; frequently referred to as the "old-fashioned bread bean," although sometimes used for soup (Plate XXXIV, figs. b 1, b 2);
   ga'huŋk (Ca. and On.);
   gana'daluk deyeyıst usahe't (Oneida);
   gana'dą doganǫstǫ'hart' usahe'ida' (Mo.).

---

[1] A general term in the Mohawk dialect spoken at Caughnawaga is dogwa'hert' uzahe'da'.

9. Buff with dark stripes, a light brown ring around the hilum; a small bean; resembles Scotia; pole, rather poor climber; a bread and soup bean; claimed as a very old Iroquois variety (Plate XXXIV, fig. b 3): tădo'gai'i (Ca.);
   atgo'a saheⁿda' (Ca.), or Wampum Bean.

10. Brownish, striped and speckled with black to brownish black; bush; long kidney-shape; resembles Speckled Wax (Plate XXXIV, figs. b 4, b 5):
    gana'daluk deyeyɪst usahe't (Oneida).

11. Striped and speckled with black and white; long, rather flat; an Iroquois hybrid (?); collected at Oneidatown (Plate XXXIV, fig. b 6).

12. Reddish brown, with dark red markings; truncated at ends; bush; resembles Best of All (Plate XXXIV, fig. c 1).

13. Dark brown, with darker stripes; broad and rather flat; pole; rather variable (Plate XXXIV, fig. c 2):
    nadaų'ia'ta' saheⁿda' (Ca.).

14. Buff, striped with maroon to nearly black; short and flat; climbing; planted with corn; claimed to be an old variety, perhaps one of the oldest (Plate XXXIV, fig. c 3):
    u'sahe'i'da' deyihä'gwayi'sda'kwa' uę'sis (On.);
    o'iä'gekaa' (Sen.)

15. Dark salmon with red to black speckles and blotches; bush (Plate XXXIV, fig. c 4):
    gana'daluk deyeyɪst usahe't (Oneida).

Soup or Corn Soup Beans.

16. Dark seal brown to nearly black ventrally and on lower end, white dorsally; bush; resembles Leopard; collected among Oneida (Plate XXXIV, fig. c 5).

17. Dull brown, a dark ring around the eye; rather long and narrow; pole; one form grown from the seed resembled Old Southern Prolific (Plate XXXIV, fig. c 6):
    ga'hio'tslɪs (Oneida).

18. Buff with maroon striping; long kidney-shape; some samples grown were pole, resembling Brockton, others bush, resembling Ruby Horticultural; also called a bread bean; collected at Oneidatown.

19. Deep brown with white at tip and somewhat dorsally; bush; Indian hybrid (?) (Plate XXXIV, fig. d 1): honodala usahe't (Oneida).

20. Scarlet Runner (*Phaseolus multiflorus*): yelano'ᴋwᴀ (Oneida).

21. A small bean, heavily blotched with maroon and buff; bush, with some runners; resembles Byer (Plate XXXIV, fig. d 2): αtgo'a (Ca.), Wampum Bean.

22. Ruby Horticultural; bush; early or medium (Plate XXXIV fig. d 3): dogwa'ɪ' (Oneida), or Cranberry.

23. Light reddish brown, with darker stripes and markings; pole; Indian hybrid (?) (Plate XXXIV, fig. d 4): honondala usahe't (Oneida).

Other Varieties (use not stated).

24. Dark brown bean; small; bush; collected at Tonawanda (Plate XXXIV, fig. d 5). oyę'gwä⁻ä' (Sen.).

25. Reddish brown, with black stripes; short, broad, and rather flat (Plate XXXIV, fig. d 6): u'sahe'i'da' unateąe'niǫ (On.).

26. Light buff, with a reddish brown ring around the eye; long, narrow, and rather pointed at ends; pole; long pods (Plate XXXIV, fig. e 1): ǫdiowas (Ca.).

27. Light fawn, blotched and finely speckled with dark red; a very short bean, with truncated ends; Cut Short; has been known horticulturally for at least seventy-five years; sometimes called Corn-hill, or Corn Bean; collected among Oklahoma Seneca by C. M. Barbeau (Plate XXXIV, fig. e 2).

Green Beans in the Pod—*gatgwędai'stia'gɩ'* (On.).

Green beans in the pod may be cooked, while fresh, and made into a soup. In preparing this, the pods are cut into pieces and boiled until tender. Fresh milk, also butter and salt, are added. The two recipes last mentioned have become very popular among the whites.

Another way of cooking green beans in the pod is to cook them whole, without slicing. The red cranberry bean is usually chosen. When done, they are taken by the stem, the head is thrown back, the pod taken into the mouth and drawn between the teeth, leaving the strings or fibres behind.

A slightly different way is to boil the pods until tender, then add butter and seasoning. A name given for the latter was u'sahe'i'da'se'i' gatgwę'du' (On.).

Green Beans Shelled—*v'sahe'da'se'* (On.).

The beans are taken when fully formed, but not yet ripe, placed in a pot, boiled, and seasoned to suit the taste.

Fried Beans—*ga'sahe'do'gwa' gasahedagęi'da'wɩ' o'na'gɩ'* (On.).

Green beans in the pod are first boiled until tender. Then they are fried in bear or sunflower oil. Butter would be a modern substitute.

Beans with Corn—*v'sahe'da'se' ga'sahe'i'du' unęha'se'gɩ'* (On.).

In this recipe, green, shelled beans are boiled with green sweet corn. Meat may be added. The preparation is then seasoned with salt, pepper, and butter or fat.

Soup of Dried Beans—*a'yuk u'gwę'da'si' gaha'di'* (On.).

Green beans in the pod are also prepared by boiling, drying in evaporating baskets or on a flat board, and storing away in a bag or barrel. When required for use, they are soaked, then boiled in the usual way, after which butter and seasoning are added. Cranberry beans are favoured.

Beans and Squash—u'ni·ǫsa'odji·sgwa' (On.).

Green beans in the pod are cooked with squash cut up into small pieces. This is considered a very old way.

A variant of this is to cook cranberry beans in the pod, and, when they are nearly dry, to serve them in the shell of a boiled squash.[1]

Green Beans with Meat—ga'negageiⁿtcäniⁿ hega'waheiⁿwiᶜ (On.).

Green pod beans are cut into small pieces, then placed in the pot along with some kind of meat, such as pork or beef.

Sweet Soup—usahe'da'gei' (On.).

Ripe shelled beans are washed with hot water; those that float and are bad are picked out; the remainder are cooked until soft; sugar is then added to make a sweet soup.

Mashed Beans—gadjisgǫⁿniᶜ u'sahe'i'da' (On.).

Beans are often cooked "like potatoes," to use the expression of an informant, then mashed with a masher or pounder. The dish is also called u'sahe'i'da' o'dji'sgwa' (On.).

Beans Mixed with Bread.

Beans are very frequently—in fact, usually—mixed with corn bread, although other materials are occasionally used. The beans are first cooked just so that they are a little firm and will remain whole. They are then mixed with corn bread paste and again cooked in the making of the bread.

---

[1] Parker, A. C., *Bulletin 144, New York State Museum*, p. 90.

Bean Soup—u'sahe'da'gei' (On.).[1]

The ripe beans are boiled with meat and stirred and mashed with a paddle until they are thoroughly mixed. The meat used may be beef, venison, or any other kind.

Other Terms (On.).

Bean pole, o'änoda'kwa' ʋsahe'i'da'.
Bean vine, ʋ'sahe'i'da' uɛˣsa'.
Bean pod, ʋ'sahe'i'da' utgwɛ'da'.
The string in a pod, utgwɛ'da' u'gɯ'ää'.
Stem of a pod, sa'nǫ diyuniǫ'da'.

Explanation of Terms.

dogwa'ɪ' (Oneida) ⎫
dogwa'herɩ' (Mo.). ⎬ a cranberry.
αˣyuk (On.) ⎪
haˣyuk (Ca.) ⎭

u'sahe'i'da' (On.) ⎫
osahe'ida' (Mo.) ⎬ a bean.
usahe'ɩ (Oneida) ⎪
saheˣda' (Ca.) ⎭

uɛ'sis (On.), climbing.
dji'tgwa' (On.), yellow.
utgwɛ'da' (On.), red.
oyɛ'gwä̈ạ̈' (Sen.), smoky-coloured, brown.
ga'huŋk (On.), a wild goose.
gana'daluk (Oneida) ⎫ bread.
gana'dą̈ (Mo.) ⎭
deyihä'gwayi'sda'kwa' (On.), mixed with bread.
deyeyɩst (Oneida), mixed with.
αtgo'a (Ca.), wampum.

---

[1] Seneca, usai'i'dagi'.

CUCURBITACEÆ OR VINE FOODS.

Many varieties of *Cucurbitaceæ*, including pumpkins, squashes, cucumbers, and melons, were cultivated by the Iroquois and are the subject of frequent mention historically, although, unfortunately, they are not always described so that we can determine the species.

Most of the *Cucurbitaceæ* are considered to be of American origin, the exceptions being the water-melon, some of the varieties of cucumber, and, possibly, also *Cucurbita maxima*, of which the Hubbard squash is a type, and which are thought to have been imported after the discovery.[1] Cartier enumerates at least three species of *Cucurbitaceæ*. Hariot, in 1586, found growing in Virginia a number of kinds of "pompions, melons, and gourds." Beverly, also, mentions the "cushaws," which he describes as "a kind of Pompion of a bluish-green Colour, streaked with white, when they are fit for Use. They are larger than the Pompions and have a long narrow Neck." "Macocks" are defined by the same writer as "a sort of Melopepones, or lesser sort of Pompion, of these they have a great Variety; but the Indian Name Macock serves for all."[2] "Smith's Voyages" also differentiates between "pompions and macocks." Brickell, "History of North Carolina," enumerates "Gourds, Mellons, Cucumbers, Squashes, Semblens."[3] In a general way, the term pompion or pumpion seems to have been applied to the forms of *Cucurbita pepo* which we call pumpkins; and macock, cushaw, and symnel or semblen to those which are commonly referred to as squashes.[4] The symnel is considered to have been the scalloped squash.

---

[1] Sturtevant, *History of Garden Vegetables*, Amer. Nat., vol. XXIII, p. 673.

[2] Beverly, *History*, vol. II, p. 27.

[3] Brickell, *History of North Carolina*, p. 289.

[4] De Candolle, *Origin of Cultivated Plants*, p. 252, considers macock and cushaw as referring to pumpkins and quotes Dr. Harris, *American Journal*, 1857, vol. XXIV, p. 441, and Trumbull, *Bull. of Torrey Bot. Club*, 1876, vol. VI, p. 69, in support of this view. De Candolle asserts, conservatively, that "all that we learn . . . is that the natives a century after the discovery of Virginia and twenty to forty years after its colonization by Sir Walter Raleigh, made use of some fruits of the Cucurbitaceæ."

Josselyn, in "New England Rarities," refers to the "Squashes, but more truly squoutersquashes, a kind of mellon or rather gourd; for they sometimes degenerate into gourds. Some of these are green; some yellow; some longish, like a gourd; others round like an apple; all of them pleasant food, boyled and buttered and seasoned with spice. But the yellow squash—called an apple squash (because like an apple) and about the bigness of a pome water—is the best kind."[1]

Aboriginal squashes are everywhere referred to as having been delicious. The Relation of 1656-57 states that among the dainties which were served up by the early Onondagas were "the beans and squashes of the country, which are firmer and better than those of France." Le Jeune, 1636, informs us that "the squashes last sometimes four and five months, and are so abundant that they are to be had almost for nothing, and so good that, on being cooked in the ashes, they are eaten as apples are in France."[2] Squashes, in fact, often formed the principal food at certain seasons,[3] and were not only kept fresh, but were cut into strips and placed in evaporating trays; or strung upon cords suspended near the fireplace until dry, then stored away. Squashes are also said to have been placed in storage pits, along with other garden products, and dug out from time to time as occasion required.[4]

Suggestions of the ceremonial importance of the squash are frequent. Feasts, such as those in response to dreams, were often made from it.[5] It is also eaten in present-day longhouse ceremonies. The squash rattles used by the Medicine Societies are most frequently made from the long-handled calabash or gourd (*Lagenaria vulgaris*), although such squashes as the summer crookneck and the old-fashioned hard-shelled varieties were sometimes used.

---

[1] Josselyn, *New England Rarities*, p. 89.
[2] *Jesuit Relations*, R. G. Thwaites ed., vol. X, p. 103.
[3] Ibid., vol. LXVII, p. 213; vol. XXVII, p. 65.
[4] Mrs. John Gibson (Ca.) and other informants confirm this statement. Ibid., vol. LVII, p. 251.
[5] Ibid., vol. LVII, p. 251.

On some occasions, as a result of over-eating, squashes seem to have been the cause of severe intestinal disturbances. Heckewelder observed "that these fevers break out nearly always in the wild plum season, . . . sometimes, also, after a long famine or deprivation of food; when they eat to excess the green corn, squashes (courges) and other watery vegetables."[1] Similar references are to be found elsewhere. The Relations note that few died of this complaint.[2]

A number of the older people still cultivate a few of these old-fashioned squashes, of which specimens were obtained on several of the reservations. One of these resembled a very small pumpkin; the other was a rather small, marrow-like squash, very variable in form and producing five or six distinct varieties from the same seed. The varieties were round to oblong and from dark green to dark green with stripes of a lighter shade. None of these were referable to commonly known seedstore varieties.

Squashes were commonly planted in the hills of corn, the two kinds of seed being dropped in together.[3] Pumpkins were grown in a similar manner. Melons might be grown in some sheltered clearing, where there was sufficient sunlight to make them ripen.

Varieties of Cucurbitaceæ[4] *(Onondaga Names).*

The small, pumpkin-like squash: uʻniǫsa'ǫ'wɩʻ udji'tgwa' ni'yut; onaǫslaǫ'wɛʻ (Oneida).
The small, variable, marrow-like squash: uʻniǫ'sa'ǫ'wɩʻ.
Marrow (common): uʻniǫ'sa'ǫ'wɩʻ uʻniǫ'sɩs (squash, long).
Summer crookneck: uʻgⱳ'ää' uʻniǫ'sa'ǫ'wɩʻ.

---

[1] Heckewelder, *History*, p. 355.

[2] *Jesuit Relations*, R. G. Thwaites ed., vol. LXIV, p. 177.

[3] Squashes, in some places, are planted early in hot beds, then transplanted; in earlier times they are said also to have been started indoors.

[4] The Cucurbitaceæ are classified botanically as pumpkin, vegetable marrow, summer crookneck, scalloped squash: *Cucurbita pepo*; Hubbard squash: *Cucurbita maxima*; winter crookneck: *Cucurbita moschata*; watermelon, citron: *Cucumis citrullus*; muskmelon: *Cucumis melo*; cucumber: *Cucumis sativus*.

Scalloped squash: u'nu'skahe'dǫ' u'niǫ'sa'ǫ'wɩ'.

Pumpkin: u'niǫso'wanę's wadę'ses (dragging it along); nowadays the first word only is used; oneyzerago'a (Mo., Caughnawaga).

Hubbard squash: dega'niǫ'sa'si'haa'.

Winter crookneck: dega'niǫ'sa'si'haa' onagⁿaa' (horn).

Water-melon: niǫsagaⁿdɩ'(melon to eat raw).

Citron: ena'djiu'tha' niǫsagaⁿdɩ' (cooking melon).

Muskmelon: wahia'.is (getting ripe).

Cucumber: udnǫskai'äniɩ'.

Boiled Squash—wae'niǫsu' (On.).

Cut the squash into halves; wrap in basswood leaves and place in a kettle; add a little water; boil for two hours; remove leaves, and place on a wooden or bark dish (u'sǫda'); eat without further preparation.

Squash Baked in Ashes—wade'niǫsǫ'da'gwa' o'gähägǫ'wa' (On.).

The whole squashes are placed under hot coals and cinders, obtained by kindling a large fire in the open, or in an old-fashioned fire-place. The ashes are then washed off and the squashes served. Another name applied is wade'niǫ'syⁿda" (On.).

Mashed Squash—u'niǫ'sa' u'dji'sgwa' (On.).

Take the squashes when sufficiently mature, cut into small pieces, boil, and mash. Eat with butter and a little sugar. In olden times deer suet and maple sugar were used. Any squash may be cooked in this manner.

Squash Used in Bread-Making.

Old-fashioned squashes (uniǫ'sa'ǫ'wɩ' u'niǫsee'dji's) are cut into small pieces, boiled and mashed, then mixed into the paste when making corn bread. Dried squash may be boiled and mashed and used in the same way.

Dried Squash.

In the autumn, among the Canadian Onondaga, squashes are frequently cut into narrow pieces lengthwise, then dried over the stove in flat evaporating trays or baskets.

In preparing them for use, the dried strips are washed in warm water, soaked, then boiled and eaten with butter. The strips are called una'ǫ'gaa' (On.).

Pumpkin Sauce—ʋ'niǫsu'wanɛ's u'dji'sgwa' (On.).

Pumpkins are cut into pieces, boiled, mashed, then sweetened and served for eating.

Pumpkin is also cut into pieces and dried for use in winter. When required for eating, it is washed, boiled, mashed, and sweetened. A little lard may also be added. According to an Oneida recipe, the dried pumpkin may be boiled with meat to the consistency of "potato soup."

Pumpkin with Beans—ga'niǫsuʳwiˊ tca'gatgwę'du' (On.).

Cut the pumpkins, when fresh, into pieces; boil, adding green beans shelled and cooking them along with it; add butter and salt.

Preserved Cucumbers—dega'niǫsa'hiyuⁿdjisdɩˊ (On.).

Cucumbers are said to have been preserved by washing and placing them in a brine made with salt and sheep sorrel,[1] deyaguʻnaʳdjiɑks (On.), the sorrel being placed at the top and bottom. Quite a bit of the latter was used. A board with a stone on it was placed on top of the contents, which were allowed to stand for a couple of weeks. Pickles prepared in this way were considered a great delicacy. This was probably a European recipe.

Fried Squash.

The squash is cut into quarters, placed in a bread pan, and put on the stove or in the oven to fry. Squash cooked in this way is either sweetened or seasoned with salt, pepper, and butter.

---

[1] Sheep sorrel, *Rumex acetosella*.

Dried Pumpkin Sauce—u'niǫsɑ'thą u'dji'sgwa' u'na'u'ŋgaa' (On.).

A quantity of dried pumpkin is placed in the corn-pounder and pounded, sifted to a fine meal or flour, boiled, and sweetened, after which grease is added.

Baked Pumpkin—wa'dɪksu''da' (On.).

The dried pumpkin is pounded, sifted, then soaked in cold water for an hour to an hour and a half. It is then sweetened and grease added. A pan is greased, the pumpkin placed in it, marked with a knife into cakes, and baked in the oven.

Cornmeal and Pumpkin—u'dji'sgwa' (On.).

The pumpkin is sliced, boiled, sugar is added, also Indian corn meal to make a pudding. This is eaten with sugar and milk.

Historical Foods.

Mention is made historically of a number of ways of preparing pumpkins and squashes. Sagard refers to them as an ingredient of "eschionque," which consists of a "soup in which one has first cooked some shredded meat or fish, together with a quantity of squash, if so desired." This was thickened with a meal made of parched, dried corn.

For ordinary "sagamité," or "ottet" (Huron), unparched corn was ground to a flour and, without sifting, made into a soup with some sort of meat. During the squash season, squashes were frequently cut into pieces and added to the mixture.[1]

Cooking squashes under the ashes was common and seems to have been a favourite method when open fire-places were in vogue.

Squash flowers were sometimes used, though little recollection of this seems to exist at present. Upon the occasion of a visit paid by Bartram to Onondaga, in 1743, there was served

---

[1] Sagard, *Voyage,* vol. I, p. 96.

a "kettle full of young squashes and their flowers boiled in water, and a little meal mixed." Bartram considered this "but weak food."[1] The sterile or staminate flowers were employed.

The Relation of 1638-39 states that "the usual sauce with the food is pure water, juice of corn or of squashes."

LEAF, STEM, AND BARK FOODS.

Extensive use was made by the Iroquois of the vegetative parts of various plants, trees, and shrubs. They were in many cases considered great delicacies and were usually collected in the earlier part of the season, while young and tender. Many of them are still in use and include the following, which are cooked like spinach and seasoned with salt, pepper, or butter.

Milkweed, *Asclepias syriaca*, uä'gwę'sda' (On.), or tganǫhäⸯsahi's (On., "milk comes out"), utshe'wa'nda (Mo.), ganǫ'kwais (Ca.); used in three ways:

1. The young plants, stem and leaves.
2. When the stem becomes a little more mature, the leaves only are used.
3. The immature flower clusters.

Plants with white leaves should not be used. These are o'tgǫ (On., "witch"). Informant, J. Jamieson, jun.

Waterleaf, *Hydrophyllum virginianum*, uätsgąⸯda' (On.), u'si'iuks (On.), ora'sgɛ'ęda' (Mo.): the leaves or young plants.

Marsh marigold, *Caltha palustris*, ganawaha'ks (On., "makes a hole in the swamp"), gänawaha's (Ca.).

Yellow dock, *Rumex crispus*, die'da' (On.), i'diedę (Mo.), ganu'da' (Ca.): the young leaves, before the stem appears.

Pigweed, *Chenopodium album*, ganadanǫⸯwi' (On.), skanadanụ'wɩ' (Mo.), gwɩ'sgwɩs gadiwano'gras (Ca., "pig eats it").

Lamb's quarters, *Amaranthus retroflexus* (Onondaga name same as preceding), diunheⸯgǫ (Ca.).

Mustard, *Brassica*, various species, more particularly *B. nigra*, udji'tgwa' niawęhuⸯdą (On.).

---

[1] Bartram, *Journal*, p. 59.

118

Purslane, *Portulaca oleracea*, udji'nowanhe"da' (On.), nonia-gai'i'i' uhiägwi'ia' (On., "partridge toes"), daksai'dɑs usi"da' (Ca., "chicken feet"), udja'sgwę'da' (Ca.).

Dandelion, *Taraxicum officinale*, udji'tgwa' niawęhu'dą̈ (On., "yellow flower"), odji'n'gwɑl˙ niyudji'djo^DŲ (Oneida), ugahą̈do'niǫ (Ca., "holes in the stem").

Burdock, *Arctium Lappa*, unǫgwa˙si'wanɛ's (On.): the young leaves are used.

Nettle, *Urtica dioica*, gohe"cra's (Ca.)

Skunk cabbage, *Symplocarpus fœtidus* (Mo. o'se'dǫ'): (Ca., unra'dowa'nɛs ganǫ"sagras); the young leaves and shoots.

Leek, *Allium tricoccum*, u'nǫ'sa' gǫda˙dowäni'yu' (On., "onion wild").

Wild garlic, *Allium canadense*, u'nǫ'sa' ga'nǫsuha'ha' (On.).

Wood betony, *Pedicularis canadensis*, and *P. lanceolata*, gwe"dis (Ca.), gwę̨'dis (On.).

Sensitive fern, *Onoclea sensibilis*, dwa'hųdes gananitsga'-kwa' (Ca., "deer, what they lie on"), uni'suwɛkwa' (On., "bait").

A number of plants, such as the sheep sorrel, purslane, dandelion, water-cress, burdock, yellow dock, the mustards, and pigweed, are considered to be European introductions, a further illustration of the readiness of the Iroquois in the adoption of new materials.

Other plants are said to have been eaten raw, in some cases with salt. These include:

Watercress, *Radicula nasturtium-aquaticum*, ınä"dɑks (On.), diusai"dawit (Ca., "pepper, tastes like").

Peppermint, various species, u'nai'yunt (Ca.).

Oxalis, *Oxalis corniculata*, deyuhiyu"djis awɛnu"gää' (On., "sour plant")

Sheep sorrel, *Rumex acetosella*, ųsu'tha' utgwę"da' niyut (On., "paint, red, like").

Leek and wild garlic. The bulbs, consisting of the fleshy bases of the leaves, are also eaten raw.

Among the foods derived from the bark or branches of trees, shrubs, and woody vines are:

Grapevine, *Vitis vulpina*, u'niǫgwi"sää' (On.): the fresh
shoots are eaten, without peeling.

Sumac, *Rhus glabra*, utgo"da' (On.): the fresh shoots peeled
and eaten raw.

Red Raspberry, *Rubus aculeatissimus*, na'djiu"gwa' (On.);
the fresh shoots are peeled and eaten.

Pine, *Pinus strobus*, and others, u'na"da' (On.), u'ne'dago'wa
(Mo., white pine), gaiyųdara'gǫ (Mo., white pine).

Cornstalk: sections are cut between the joints and chewed
to quench the thirst; said to have a sweet taste.

Bark of the soft maple, *Acer rubra* and *A. saccharinum*,
awęha'tgwa (On.); the bark is dried beside the fire, then
pounded in the mortar, sifted, and made into a bread;
said not to taste badly.

Bark of the hard or sugar maple,[1] *Acer saccharum*, uhwa"da'
(On.): is used in the same way as the preceding.

Deer excrement was, until quite recently, gathered and made
into a soup by itself, or a small quantity was tied up in a cloth
and placed with the corn when the latter was half cooked. This
is said to have been "strong stuff." It seems to have been somewhat of the nature of an emergency food, or one used principally
by poor people. Informants: David Jack and John Jamieson,
jun.

ROOT FOODS.

Roots[2] of various wild and cultivated plants were evidently
used extensively and a few, such as the wild potato, the arti-
choke, and the pepper-root, are still eaten by some of the older
people.

The roots of the yellow pond-lily, Solomon's seal, the Indian
turnip, and skunk cabbage are referred to as having been used
in the Iroquois area, but have been practically forgotten by
present-day Iroquois.

---

[1] Used also by neighbouring Algonkin tribes, such as the Montagnais.
See *Jesuit Relations*, R. G. Thwaites ed., vol. VI, pp. 271, 273.

[2] On., ukde'ha'.

The common potato, although a native to America,[1] was a comparatively recent introduction among the eastern woodlands tribes, arriving there with the general adoption of European products. The tubers of the *Apios tuberosa* are often referred to as potatoes and are sometimes planted in suitable locations, though they are not, strictly speaking, cultivated. A couple of interesting old varieties of potatoes were obtained from Alexander Snider of Tonawanda. These are described in the list of roots appended.

> Crinkle root or pepper root, *Dentaria diphylla*, ɪkde′hɛks (On.): eaten raw with salt. Some boil them. A Mohawk recipe is to wash the roots and add vinegar. Also *Dentaria laciniata*, ukde′huwi (Ca.).
>
> Groundnut, or wild potato, *Apios tuberosa*, ho′nonda' (Ca.), unänuⁿgwa' (On.), gwɛhɥwɛnɛ′ha' o′nena′da' (Mo., "Indian potato").
>
> Burdock, *Arctium Lappa*, onǫgwaˈsi′wanɛ's (On.). The roots were dried by the fire, then stored away for winter use. To prepare them, they were soaked and boiled to a sort of soup.
>
> Claytonia, or spring beauty, *Claytonia virginica*, ganɛnuˈgǫ′ta' (On.).
>
> Artichoke, *Helianthus tuberosus*, unänuⁿgwa' (On.): used raw, boiled, or fried.
>
> Potato, *Solanum tuberosum*, hononda'ǫ′wi (Ca., "old-fashioned potato"), onɑ′nạ'da' (Sen.).

Two very old varieties of potato, cultivated by Alexander Snider, Seneca, of Tonawanda, were: the "Merino," a reddish-coloured potato, medium size, rather long and with deep eyes, Seneca name nɑ′nạ'des or "long potato"; the "horn" potato (Sen., onǫⁿgää' onɑ′nạ'da', or "horn potato"), small in size, elongated and tapering to one end, like a small horn; skin, dark purplish, considered to be especially suitable for baking.

---

[1] Sturtevant, *Kitchen Garden Esculents*, p. 542.
De Candolle, *Origin of Cultivated Plants*, p. 49.

GENERAL BOTANICAL TERMS.

Plant (of any kind), odjigo"djia' (On.), awɛnu"gää' (On.).
Plant (growing in bush), ga'hagǫha" awɛnu"gää' (On.).
Vine, uɛ'sɩs (On.).
Bush, ohǫ'da' (On.).
Sapling, uwɛnawɛ" (On.).
Tree, nigaie'nda'sɑ' (On.), krai'et (Ca.).
Large tree, gaiendowa'nɛ (On.).

EDIBLE FUNGI (*On.*, *unä'sa'*; *Ca.*, *unra"sa'*).

A number of kinds of fungi are used by the Iroquois, and
were probably employed even more extensively in former times.
Among the kinds enumerated by informants were:

Common mushroom, *Agaricus campestris*, unä'sa' (On.),
anahau'tra' (Ca., "hat" or "cap"), e'skɑn agohy"da'
(Mo., "ghost's ears").
Morel, *Morchella*, several species, uya'gä"da' (On., "penis"),
ohǫ"da' (Ca., "ear").
Puffball, *Lycoperdon giganteum* and other species, duwatage-
hänegąus (Ca., "smoke shoots out"), o'tgy raona'daro
(Mo., "devil's bread"), dewadi'ɛ'gwae'gwas onä"sa'
(On., "smoking fungus"), deyutwi'no'ni's unä'sa' (On.
"round fungus").

John Jamieson, jun., stated that it is not a good thing to
eat the puffball, as one will become jealous. The name he gave
for the fungus was utsɔ"gwa' (On.).

Polyporus fungi, various species,[1] unra"sa' (Ca.), unä'sa'
(On.). These were most commonly boiled, or used as an
ingredient of soups. One informant stated that they were boiled

---

[1] According to Chief Gibson, the edible Polyporus fungi are differentiated
according to the kind of tree on which they grow. Those growing on maples
are uhwa''da' unä'sa'; on hickories, unänu'gaa unä'sa'; on swamp oaks,
ganawagǫ'ha' unä'sa'; on white oaks, gaądagä'äda' unä'sa'; on red oaks,
gai'ɩ'di' unä'sa'. A Polyporus found growing on rotten pine stumps is called
unä'sa' ukdjinudo'niǫ netu" unä'sudo'niǫ ("fungus on rotten stump growing").
A number of the Polyporus fungi are edible, including *P. frondosus*, *P. pini-
cola*, *P. sulphureus*. The last was described accurately by the same informant.

for a few minutes, then drained and boiled again until thoroughly done. At present they are frequently fried in butter and seasoned as required.

Fried Mushroom—ganäsage'i'da'wi' (*On.*).

Bring a kettle of water to a boil, add the mushrooms (Polyporus or other kinds), boil for ten or fifteen minutes, drain; then fry the mushrooms in butter or grease, with a little water added, seasoning as desired. The common mushroom and the puffball are first peeled, then cooked as described.

Mushroom Soup—unä'sa' u'nega'gei' On.).

Boil the mushrooms as described in the preceding recipe, drain, add more hot water and also some kind of meat, such as pork; boil until the meat is cooked.

NUTS AS FOOD (NUT, U'SU"GWA', ON.).

A considerable variety of edible nuts are met with throughout the Iroquois country and were not only eaten raw, but were also incorporated into other foods. At present they are usually cracked and eaten as a treat during the winter.

The gathering of nuts was usually left to the women and children, who gathered the harvest after the frosts had brought it down. The hickory nut seems to have been the most widely esteemed.

The acorn was used quite commonly, probably more particularly the sweet kinds, such as those of the white oak (*Quercus alba*), the chestnut oak (*Quercus Prinus*), and some others. Even the bitter acorns of the red and black oak were used in times of necessity, and also the nuts of the bitter hickory. The Hurons are said to have prepared them by "first boiling them in a lye made from ashes, in order to take from them their excessive bitterness."[1] According to another writer "they (the

---

[1] *Jesuit Relations*, R. G. Thwaites ed., vol. XXXV, p. 99.

Hurons) also make provision of acorns, which they boil in several waters to remove the bitterness, and consider them very good."[1]

Nut-cracking outfits, consisting of a couple of rounded stones with pitted centres, were used in removing the shells. Many of the older people still remember these and a few specimens are occasionally found.

Nuts Used by Iroquois:

Hickory, *Carya ovata*, unänu'gaa (On., "shell bark"), onendoga'a' (Ca.).

Bitter hickory, *Carya cordiformis*, oso^{v}gwadji'wagä (On., "bitter nut"), unqa'dęs (Ca.).

Walnut, *Juglans nigra*, deyutsu^{v}gwagwi^{n}noni' (On., "round nut"), nyugwagwi'noni^c (Ca.).

Butternut, *Juglans cinerea*, sa^{c}su^{n}gwis or dju^{c}so^{n}gwıs (On., "long nut"), uge'hwa' (Ca.).

Hazelnut, common, *Corylus americana*, niyuhagwa'ha ustu'tshä' (On.), uso'witra' (Ca.); beaked, *Corylus rostrata*, u'hıs ustu'tshä' (On.).

Beechnut, *Fagus grandifolia*, utsgä^{n}ä'.

Chestnut, *Castanea dentata*, uheya^{n}da' (On.), uhi'da' (Ca.).

Acorns:

Swamp oak, *Quercus bicolor*, ganawagqha' u^{c}su^{n}gwa' (On.).

White oak, *Quercus alba*, gai^{c}t^{c}di' u^{c}su^{n}gwa' (On.), gaga^{n}da' (Ca.).

Red oak, *Quercus rubra*, go'wi^c (Ca.).

The Chestnut oak (*Quercus Prinus*) was probably included.

Nuts Used in Bread-making.

A Cayuga informant[2] stated that the older people used to crush the meats of the hickory, walnut, butternut, and chest-

---

[1] Sagard, *Voyages*, vol. I, p. 97.
[2] Wife of late Chief John Gibson, Grand River reservation.

nut, and mix them with the cornmeal for bread. Beans or berries were also added in the usual way. Any kind of nut, except acorns, might be used.

Nut-meat Gravy.

The meats of the hickory, walnut, and several others, were pounded, boiled slowly in water, and the oil skimmed off into a bowl. The oil was boiled again and seasoned with salt. This was used with bread, potatoes, pumpkin, squash, and other foods.

Nut-meat oil was often added to the mush used by the False-face Societies. The oil was also formerly used (like sunflower oil) for the hair, either alone or mixed with bear's grease. Lafitau remarks that the mixture was used as a preventive of mosquitoes.

Nut-meat with Potatoes.

The meats left after skimming off the oil were often seasoned and mixed with mashed potatoes.

Nut-meats in Hominy and Corn Soup.

Nut-meats were also crushed and added to hominy and corn soup to make it rich. This was described by several informants.

That this method was common in the Iroquois area is suggested by Hariot, who states that "besides their eating of them after our ordinary maner, they break them with stones and pound them in morters with water to make a milk which they use to put into some sorts of their spoonemeat; also among their sodden wheat, peaze, beanes and pompions which maketh them have a farre more pleasant taste."

Other Terms (On.).

Shuck (outer covering), o'kda'; also applied to the shell.
Nut-meat, u'nie'ɛ'.
A spoiled meat, uhetgɛⁿi'.
An empty or shrivelled nut, odjiⁿswą̈.
Nutting-time, utci'sa'io'nɛ.

I shuck the nuts, wa'gekduⁿtca'.
I crack nuts, degatsoⁿgiɑks.
The nuts are ripe, utci'saⁿi'.
I gather nuts, ksoⁿgwanǫ'gwę's.

FRUITS USED AS FOODS.

Berries and wild fruits generally have always been favourite aboriginal foods and were found in profusion in all parts of the Iroquois area. Bressani refers to the use by the Hurons of "strawberries, of two sorts; the blackberries, which grow on briars; the hazelnuts, and certain haws, and the wild plum. The walnuts have scarcely anything but the shell, and the cherries are no larger than a pea,—being little else than stone and skin, and very sour. There are some wild vines (grapes?), but in small quantity, nor are they esteemed by the Barbarians themselves; but do they esteem highly a certain fruit of violet colour, the size of a juniper berry (the blueberry?)"[1] Le Jeune states that "strawberries, raspberries and blackberries are to be found in almost incredible quantities. We gather plenty of grapes, which are fairly good."[2] Among the fruits elsewhere referred to are the cranberry, mandrake, and pawpaw,[3] the latter being found in southern Ontario, New York state, and southward.

Following the discovery, a number of European products were quickly adopted. The records of Sullivan's campaign of 1779 repeatedly refer to the orchards of apple, peach, and other kinds of fruit trees found, as well as to the general advancement of the Iroquois in horticulture. The pear and cultivated cherry were also introduced.

Among the earliest berries to ripen is the strawberry, which is followed closely by the raspberry and others. These welcome events are celebrated by longhouse ceremonies in which thanks are given, while quantities of the fruit are eaten in the feasts which follow.

---

[1] *Jesuit Relations*, R. G. Thwaites ed., vol. XXXVIII, p. 243.
[2] Ibid., vol. X, p. 103.
[3] Ibid., vol. XLIII, p. 257.

A number of special utensils were connected with the collection and preservation of fruits. Small splint baskets for picking are attached to the waist in front by means of a cord passed through the handle (Plate XXXV, figs. c, d, e). The smaller baskets are then emptied into larger pack baskets lined with freshly-plucked basswood leaves (Plate XXXV, fig. f). Bark receptacles for picking were probably common formerly

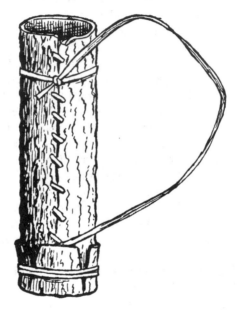

Figure 2.   Berry picking basket of elm bark, used by Mrs. John Williams, Caughnawaga.

(Fig. 2).   As in the collection of many food materials, the picking of berries was the women's and children's employment.

Gooseberries were freed from prickles by tying them up in the skin of an animal, and later in an ordinary grain-bag. They were then rubbed until the prickles were broken off.

Berries not required for immediate consumption are dried. This may be done in several ways.   The fruit may be spread out just as it is upon boards or in flat evaporating baskets (Plate XXXV, figs. a, b), and dried in the sun or by the fire; or it may be mashed and afterwards placed in small cakes upon large basswood leaves to dry. It may also be cooked and afterwards preserved in the manner just described. It is finally stored away in elm bark boxes or covered baskets.

Bartram, in a journey to the Iroquois country, describes the drying of huckleberries as follows: "This is done by setting four forked sticks in the ground, about three or four feet high, then others across, over them the stalks of our common Jacea or Saratula, on these lie the berries, as malt is spread on the hair cloth over the kiln." Underneath this was kindled a "smoke fire."[1] Kalm and other writers refer to similar methods.[2]

When wanted for use, the cakes of dried berries are soaked in warm water and cooked as a sauce, or mixed with corn bread. The dried berries were often taken along as a hunting food.

Principal Varieties.

Strawberry, *Fragaria virginiana*, uhŭdadeka᷈gwa' (On.), geniyuhŭde'sha' (Mo.).

Wood strawberry, *Fragaria vesca*, var. *americana*, uhǫ'dɩs uhŭdadeka᷈gwa' (On., "tall strawberry"), dji'sǫ'dak ganadowäni'yu' (Ca., "strawberry, wild").

Red raspberry, *Rubus idaeus* var. *aculeatissimus*, una'-djiu᷈gwa' (On.), skanegwǫdara'nŭ (Mo.).

Black raspberry, *Rubus occidentalis*, ugahe'i'gwa' (On., "small pieces"), tǫ'daktǫ (Ca., "bushes leaning over"), or swę'dąi niyu'yu'dą (Ca., "black fruit").

Dwarf raspberry, *Rubus triflorus*, uhŭdadeka᷈gwa' ogahe᷈-gwa' (On., "berry with big eyes").

Thimbleberry, *Rubus canadensis*, s'a᷈yɩs (On., "long fruit") sa'yɛzɩ' (Mo.), nęnǫ (Ca.).

Purple flowering raspberry, *Rubus odoratus*, go'danuwę'kwa' (On., "makes costive"); berry not considered edible; the root used as a remedy in diarrhœa.

Wild gooseberry, *Ribes*, various species, tcɩ'wę'dǫ'dǫ' or ɒtce'hwę᷈da' (On.).

---

[1] Bartram, *Observations*, p. 73.
[2] Kalm, *Travels*, vol. II, p. 101.

Wild black currant, *Ribes floridum*, u'sǫ'da' skah"ǫskahǫ' (On.), ona'daao'hi' (Mo.).

dju'eä'gɑk gǫ'hiɑks (On., "raccoon eats the berries").

Wild red currant, *Ribes triste*, skahǫ"skahǫ' utgwę"daa' (On., "currant, red").

Blueberry or huckleberry, early, *Vaccinium pennsylvanicum*, also *Gaylussacia baccata*, uhia'dji' niyuhu'ndagwaha (On.).

Late blueberry, *V. corymbosum* (?), uhia'dji' uhǫ'dıs (On., "blueberry, tall").

Cranberry, *V. oxycoccus* and *V. macrocarpon*, ha"yuk (On.).

Juneberry, *Amelanchier canadensis*, gä'ä'duŋk (On.), ha'duŋk (Ca.).

Elderberry, *Sambucus canadensis*, hu's䇼ha' (On.), ora'zi (Ca.), onaa'ra'ge'ha (Mo.).

Nannyberry, *Viburnum lentago*, saiya"dis (On.), also called nęsdagwę"dę, according to one informant.

Tree cranberry, *Viburnum opulus*, var. *americana*, nęsdagwę''dę (On.), djigınǫstagwǫ"dǫ (Mo.).

Wintergreen, *Gaultheria procumbens*, diyųnia'gäs (On.).

Partridge or squaw berry, *Mitchella repens*, noniagai'i'i' gǫ'hiɑks (On., "partridge eats it"), gwezä̧' gäna"ias (Ca., "partridge eats it"), usai'sda' gǫ'hiɑks (On., "snake eats it").

Wild grape, *Vitis vulpina*, u'niǫgwi''sää' (On.), gar'ragų'ha' o'nɑ'harı' (Mo.).

Mulberry, *Morus rubra*, deyuderaha'kdǫ (Mo.).

Wild red cherry, *Prunus pennsylvanica*, ganadjie"gwa' (On.); not commonly used.

Chokecherry, *Prunus virginiana*, nia'ta"da"ni' (On.) or yatadani, diagunia"ta's (Ca.), deyagonia'dawą'ıks (Mo.).

Wild black cherry, *Prunus serotina*, e'i' (On.), erıgo'a (Mo.).

Wild plum, *Prunus americana*, twi'sǫ' (On.); *Prunus nigra*, gęhä'hä (On.).

Haws, *Crataegus pruinosa*, *submollis*, and others, djigahe" dis or djigahe'dısgo'na' (On., "for bread"), djuga'-

hi'des (Ca.), gana'daŭ'niꞌ (Ca. for one of the haws—probably *C. punctata*), o'ŋgweꞌ uᵑhia', or "man's berries" (Ca. for *C. punctata*?).

Apple, *Pyrus malus*, sowahiyu'na' (On.), zewahio'wanɛ dɔyuya'dzikɔ'a (Mo., "thɔ swɔɔt applɔ").

Crab-apple, *Pyrus coronaria*, uhiȧdji'wagą̈ (On., "sour fruit"),[1] hiȧdjiawa'gǫ (Ca.), diuwadji'stąu (Ca.).

Pear, *Pyrus communis*, utsheᵑda' u'hia' (On., "like a jug, fruit").

Peach, *Prunus persica*, gǫ'ⁿhwai'ꞌ' (On.).

Pawpaw, *Asimina triloba*; southern Ontario, New York state, and southward.

Mandrake, *Podyphyllum peltatum*, ugwa'ɛ' (On.), oskǫwi'da' (On.), unǫ'hųstɛ' (Mo.), ganyu'u' ogwa'a' (Sen., wild orange).

Ground cherry, *Physalis*, various species, dji'haꞌ u'hia' (On., "dog-berry"), gashe'wędǫta' (Sen., "bells").

Other Terms (Onondaga).

Berry-bush, u'hia' uhǫ'da'.

Blossoms, uwę'ha'.

Prickles, uhwi'kda'.

Berry-patch, wahiȧyɛ'ntwiꞌ.

Dried berries, u'hia'tä wahiataᵑdi'.

Berry seeds, uhia udie'tshä'.

Evaporating basket, uhiataᵛda'kwa' gaaᵑsää' (for drying berries, flat basket).

Berries are ripe, unę̇ꞌ uhia'iꞌ.

I pick berries, wa'gahia'goa'.

Plenty of berries, ŭwadaꞌhio'niꞌ (Ca.).

---

[1] Among the various actions ascribed to "The Evil-Minded" (Oneida, Dawi'sgaꞌl) is the creation of the crab-apple. See also Caswell, H. S., *Our Life Among the Iroquois*, p. 233.

GENERAL FOLK-LORE ITEMS.

It was stated by Alex. Snider, Tonawanda, that God[1] made the corn with plenty of oil in it. This was noticed by the Devil, who threw ashes over it, thus destroying the oily quality. According to John Jamieson, sen., corn formerly produced all the year around. You could pluck off an ear and another would grow in its place. The Devil, however, threw dirt on it and covered it over, so that it has only one season now and is not so productive.

Pines used to bear good-sized berries on the cones. The Devil looked at them and thought they were too good for the people, so he threw ashes on them and spoiled them.

The Devil noticed that walnuts were very thin-shelled— in fact, had only a thin skin over them—and also possessed very large meats. He then threw ashes over them and made the shells hard and thick and the meats small. The last two items are also by John Jamieson, sen.

A number of articles used in much the same way as chewing gum were mentioned by David Jack and John Jamieson, jun. These included: slippery-elm bark mixed with wheat; pitch from dead pines, mixed with beeswax; the bast or inner bark of the basswood; the buds of the basswood—which were said to keep one from being thirsty; the gum of the spruce (On., skanę^{n}dęs; Ca., ganę^{n}dęs); the spongy tissue found in the teats of a female deer, a material which is said to last well and to have no unpleasant taste or odour.

ANIMAL FOODS.

Lahontan remarks that "these Iroquois nations are very advantageously situated. They have a pleasant and fertile country; but they want roe-bucks and turkeys, as well as fish, of which their rivers are altogether destitute, insomuch that they are forced to fish in the lake, and to broil or dry their fish with a

---

[1] "God" and the "Devil" no doubt refer here to the deities sometimes called the "Good-minded" and the "Evil-minded," or T'harǫ'hiawä^n-k'hǫ' and Tawi'skarǫ' (names by Hewitt, *Handbook of American Indians*).

fire, in order to keep them and transport (Plates XXXVI and XXXVII) them to their villages. They are in like manner forced to range out of their territory, in quest of beaver, in the winter time, either towards Ganaraske, or to the sides of the lake of Toronto, or else towards the great river of the Outaouas."[1] The scarcity of meat or game in the Huron country is also frequently mentioned.

A wide variety of animal foods was employed and in times of scarcity the list was no doubt considerably extended. Most of the smaller mammals, birds, amphibia, and even some of the reptilia, were eaten, also many of the mollusca, crustacea, and insecta.

Kinds Prohibited or Avoided.

A number of more or less positive prohibitions or avoidances are found, though there seems to be no special connexion with totemic animals. For instance, the flesh of pregnant animals was stated by a Cayuga[2] to be "no good" and to produce diarrhœa. Animals inhabiting graveyards should not be killed for food, or "bad luck" will result. The spirits of dead people were stated by the same informant to be in these animals.

As in the case of other foods, a woman at the menstrual period is not allowed to touch meat intended for preservation or for general household purposes, otherwise it would spoil. A poisonous quality was also thought to be thus imparted to food.

In trapping such animals as the mink or muskrat, the carcass, after it has been skinned, must not be thrown upon the ground, or the animals will be offended and no longer allow themselves to be taken. A Cayuga,[3] who furnished the information, was accustomed to place the bodies in the crotch of a small tree. The Relations and other early records refer to the fact that among the Iroquois and others the bones were not allowed to be thrown to the dogs, or non-success in hunting would result.[4]

---

[1] Cf. also Charlevoix, *Voyages*, vol. III, p. 118.
Jesuit Relations, R. G. Thwaites ed, vol. LII, pp. 117, 119.
[2] John Jamieson, jun.
[3] John Jamieson, jun.
[4] *Jesuit Relations*, R. G. Thwaites ed., vol. XLIV, pp. 301, 303.

The porcupine (*Erethizon dorsalis*) is considered to possess special powers and sometimes receives the appellation of "witch." One which comes prowling around the hunter's camp should not be molested, as he brings news. A Seneca informant[1] states that he once shot one and afterward found out that a relative had died about that time.

If you handle a star-nosed mole (*Condylura cristata*), without killing him, you will be afflicted with headache and nosebleed. As a preventive, the hands should be washed at once.[2]

Some informants considered that those making a meal of turtle's meat would be a long time dying,[3] although the flesh was admitted to be good. The idea of sympathetic magic here involved is common. An Onondaga[4] was of the opinion that it was the heart only which should be avoided. It is said that the flesh was formerly eaten by warriors with a view to rendering them difficult to kill.

The wood frog (*Rana cantabrigensis*) has certain peculiar powers attributed to it. If one rescues it from danger, such as from being swallowed by a snake, it will, according to an old Oneida, [5] afterwards assist its rescuer in time of trouble or danger. An exact counterpart of this item, though throwing no more light on the origin of the idea, is found in "Our Life among the Iroquois," by Mrs. H. S. Caswell. The dried body of this frog is considered to possess a medicinal value. The tree-frog (*Hyla versicolor*) was said by an Onondaga to be a "witch." Deafness will result from hearing the cry of one of these animals which has been injured.

No one, according to a Cayuga informant,[6] should molest the young of the night-hawk (*Chordeiles virginiana*), as the old one would swoop down upon him and deafen him by "booming' in his ears.

---

[1] Alex. Snider, Tonawanda, N.Y.

[2] John Jamieson, jun.

[3] The reflex movements after death continue for a long time in the turtle-—sometimes for several days.

[4] Peter John, Brant County reserve.

[5] Anthony Day, Oneidatown, Ontario.

[6] John Jamieson, jun.

The flesh of the chickadee (*Parus atracapillus*), an extremely small bird, is popularly said, according to a Seneca informant,[1] to make any one eating it a liar. The saying is said to have originated in the story of a band of warriors who were refreshed upon the meat of a single chickadee when at the point of starvation.[2]

A number of birds and animals are, at least at present, considered uneatable on account of their disagreeable flavour, or unpopular habits of feeding.

Meat is absolutely prohibited when certain medicines are being administered, such as those possessed by the secret societies. In some cases, after such prohibition, the first meat eaten must be white meat, such as that of a white chicken.

Food which has been run over by mice, or by a small animal which seems to be the skink, *Eumeces quinquelineatus* (On., utskäi˙di'), will cause the teeth to decay and produce vomiting of blood. Children are thought to be frequently killed in this way.[3]

Other Ceremonial Usages.

Dog's[4] flesh was formerly consumed on special occasions and as a ceremonial observance. Dog feasts,[4] in fact, are said to have been offered to "Aireskoui," the Sun, who was also the god or "demon" of war, this observance securing success in war or hunting as well as the satisfactory interpretation of dreams and the recovery of the sick. The burning of the white dog at the Mid-winter Festival may be a survival of this. Stags and bears were sometimes offered in the same way.

---

[1] Chief John Gibson.

[2] One chickadee was formerly said to make meat enough for five or six. Informant, Peter John, On.

[3] John Jamieson, jun.

[4] Sagard, *Voyages*, vol. II, p. 215, remarks of the Huron dogs that they "howl rather than bark, and have straight ears like foxes; otherwise they are exactly like the medium-sized mongrels of the French villager. They serve instead of sheep, to be eaten at feasts, they harry the moose, and discover the lair of the beast, and are little expense to their masters." Regarding native dogs see Darwin, *Animals and Plants under Domestication*, vol. I, pp. 20, 21.

Ceremonial cannibalism was evidently quite a common practice, the offering in this way of prisoners captured in war being considered particularly acceptable. In some instances, according to the Relations, the Sun was thought to be offended and to withhold his favour because they had been remiss in torturing and eating prisoners. Portions of the latter, such as the heart, the lips, and other parts were apparently eaten from a belief in sympathetic magic, or the ability to acquire the bravery or other virtues of an enemy.[1]

Mammals.

The meat of the deer, bear, and the larger game animals is said to have been boiled, after which the water was changed, the meat subjected to another boiling, then removed from the pot, and fried in grease. The soup remaining was thickened with corn hulls or siftings. Whole corn was sometimes added instead.

A common way of preparing meat was to broil it on pointed sticks. It was also dried on a sort of grating of sticks placed over a fire. The fat or tallow was kept for cooking purposes.

The oil tried out in cooking the meat of bear, raccoon, porcupine, and other animals is kept and used for medicinal purposes, such as rubbing on the back and chest for "cramps" and for application to newly-born infants. Deer's tallow is particularly prized for certain purposes, such as for snow-snake "medicine," the principle involved being the familiar one of sympathetic magic.[2]

Beaver was highly appreciated, especially the tail, the flesh of the animal being used both fresh and smoked.[3]

Dried meat was sometimes boiled to soften it a little, after which it was placed in the mortar and pounded to a sort of hash, then boiled again, with the addition of grease and salt.

---

[1] *Jesuit Relations*, R. G. Thwaites ed., vol. XLI, p. 53, Le Mercier *re* Onondaga (1653-54).

Ibid., vol. X, pp. 227, 229.

Ibid., vol. XXVI, pp. 19 and 33, Vimont *re* Iroquois (1642-44).

[2] John Jamieson, jun., David Jack, and others.

[3] The use of beaver meat was described by a Seneca informant, Chief John Gibson.

The skunk, *Mephitis mephitica*, is still eaten, the meat being considered good for all kinds of ailments.[1] Other animals eaten are the woodchuck (*Arctomys monax*), the muskrat (*Fiber zibethicus*), rabbits, hares, and all kinds of squirrels.[2] The carnivorae, generally, seem to have been avoided.

Mice are said to have been used among the early Huron, though the description given is suggestive of the short-tailed vole (*Microtus Pennsylvanicus*).

Birds.

Among the principal birds eaten are: wild ducks, geese, the larger owls, the partridge, quail, woodcock, snipe, plover, black-birds, woodpeckers, the robin, the meadow-lark, and the mourning-dove. A number of others were no doubt utilized in case of necessity. Cranes are said by Loskiel to have been "seldom eaten." The loon was regarded as a "witch," and was consequently avoided.

Owls are said to taste good. They are boiled until half done, then roasted. The oil is saved as a medicine.

The wild turkey and pigeon were formerly found in Iroquois territory, but have now disappeared.

Wild birds' eggs were frequently eaten, and included those of the partridge, quail, wild duck, plover, and many others. The young birds, just ready to hatch, are said to have been highly esteemed.[3] The number of eggs in a partridge nest are said by John Jamieson, jun., to indicate how many years longer the finder will live.

Batrachians and Reptiles.

Frogs of several kinds were an article of diet,[4] particularly the larger species, such as the bullfrog (*Rana catesbiana*) and the leopard frog (*Rana pipiens*). The legs were skinned, broiled on pointed sticks, then salted and eaten.

---

[1] David Jack (Ca.).

[2] John Jamieson, jun., says that he has eaten killed squirrels, which are liked by the pigmies. He then offered tobacco to the latter and asked them for luck in hunting or other such occupations. The squirrel's body was then left upon the ground or hung up in a tree.

[3] *Jesuit Relations*, vol. XLIV, p. 299.

[4] Ibid., vol. XXXIX, p. 215.

The wood frog (*Rana cantabrigensis*) was stated by an Oneida[1] to be eaten whole. It was formerly made into a soup, though the informant preferred it fried in butter. The bodies are dried and made into a broth, which is used medicinally. Other small frogs were probably also employed.

Snakes were said by several informants to have been used in former times, though this was denied by others. Charlevois refers to the use of the rattlesnake by certain tribes, possibly including the Hurons. The meat was cooked "like fish."[2]

Turtles and turtle eggs were employed quite generally, and included such species as the snapping-turtle (*Chelydra serpentina*), the painted turtle (*Chrysemys picta*), and the wood turtle (*Clemys insculptus*).

Turtle's meat was said by Chief Gibson to be "good medicine" made into either a soup or stew. The broth is considered to be good for throat troubles, or for newly-born children.

Fish.

Fish were everywhere a favourite food (Plates XXXVIII and XXXIX), although, as in the case of other game, the supply was often limited.[3] Nearly all kinds were eaten and formed a common ingredient of hominy, corn soup, and other preparations. Even the intestines were utilized in former times, though not at present, this economy having been practised when the fish were being preserved for winter use.[3] Reference has been made elsewhere to decayed salmon as an ingredient of soups.

Eels were smoked or dried and used like fish. Mention is frequently made to these in the Relations and the accounts of early writers generally. During Bartram's visit to Onondaga, for instance, his entertainers provided "great kettles of Indian corn soup, or thin hominy, with dried eels and other fish boiled in it."[4] According to this writer, also, "they cut a stick about

[1] Anthony Day.
[2] Charlevoix, *Voyages*, pp. 125 and 209, vol. III.
[3] *Jesuit Relations*, R. G. Thwaites ed., vol. XXXIX, p. 215.
[4] Martin, *Life of Jogues*, ed. by J. G. Shea, p. 123.
[5] Bartram, *Observations*, p. 60.

three feet long, and as thick as one's thumb; they split it about a foot down, and, when the eel is gutted, they coil it between the two sides of the stick, and bind the top close which keeps the eel flat, and then stick one end in the ground before a good fire."[1]

Boiled Fish. A very simple method was to boil the fish until tender, adding salt to suit the taste.

Fish Soup—u'nega'gei' (On.). Fish of any kind is boiled in a pot with a quantity of water. It is then removed and coarse corn siftings stirred in to make a soup of a suitable consistency.

Fish and Potato Soup. When potatoes are boiled, spread the fish out on top, cover with a lid and cook. When done, remove the fish and add salt and pepper.

Fried Fish. Fish are sometimes fried in bear or deer grease, salt and pepper being added. Among the kinds mentioned as being best were some of the smaller ones, such as the stone-carriers (*Exoglossum maxillingua*) and the sticklebacks (*Gasterosteus bispinosus* and *Eucalia inconstans*).

Eels are usually fried. No grease is added, but just a little water. Sturgeon is cooked in the same way, or made the basis of corn soup, as previously stated.

Roasted Fish. The fish is cleaned and stretched open by inserting a couple of small sticks. It is then impaled on another sharp stick, which is stuck in the ground before an open fire. The fish is salted before roasting.

Dried Fish. To preserve fish, cut and clean them, rub well with salt and dry in the sun or over a fire, then place in a bark box or other receptacle.

Another method is to roast in front of the fire, then hang in the smoke from an open fire-place.

Additional terms (On.).

 Fish, udjiųⁿda'.
 The tail, uda⌃sa'.
 Fins, una‛wi'na'.
 Scales, u'sda'.
 Dried fish, gääbdjiọda'tha'di‛.

---

[1] Ibid., p. 33.

Smoked fish, gaią'gwai'kdi'.
Roast fish, ga'są'yuda'.
Fried fish, gądjio'dagą'i'dawi'.
Boiled fish, gądjio'du°gwa'.
To clean fish, gayowäda°guę.
To remove the scales, gęsdą°di'.

Crustacea.

The only crustaceans eaten by the Iroquois were the crayfish (belonging to the genus *Cambarus*). These have very little
meat upon them and are seldom bothered with at present. The
Onondaga name, udjie'iɛ', signifies "feet that pinch."

Cooking Recipes. According to one recipe, furnished by
Chief Gibson, the tails only are used. These are skinned and
fried in butter or grease.

Crayfish may also be boiled to make a soup, salt and other
seasoning being added. Another method is to make a stew of
wild onions or leeks, add the crayfish, also butter, pepper, and
salt.

A simpler way is to salt the crustaceans, impale them on
pointed sticks, plant one end of the stick in the ground, and
roast them before an open fire.

Still another way was to place them whole under the hot
ashes or cinders, then cut them open along the back and eat them.

Insect Foods.

Information was obtained regarding several insect foods,
and it is evident from historical records that a number of others
were employed.

Ants of various species are said, by an Onondaga informant,[1]
to have been eaten raw on account of the acid flavour, though
more as a luxury than as a staple.

At Onondaga Castle, N.Y.,[2] the larvæ of the seventeen-
year locust (*Cicada septendecim*) were formerly ploughed or dug

---

[1] Peter John and others.
[2] Baptist Thomas, informant.

up and roasted in a pot, without water. They were stirred while cooking and, when they were thoroughly done, a little grease was added. Some of the older people are said to make use of them still. They are considered to be "good for the health." An Onondaga name given was ogwąyuⁿda'.[1]

Historical Mention. Mention is frequently made by various writers of insect foods. Loskiel, in describing the foods of the Iroquois and the Delaware, refers to locusts, although the use of the popular name leaves us in doubt as to whether the grasshopper or the cicada is meant.[2]

Du Perron, in the Relation of 1638-39, mentions the preparation by the Hurons of "a porridge made of the meal of Indian corn and water. . . . Sometimes the savages put in pieces of cinders, to season the sagamité, at other times a handful of little waterflies, which are like the gnats of Provence; they esteem these highly and make feasts of them."[3]

Brickell, "Natural History of North Carolina," records the use of "young wasps" among the tribes of that area.

Sagard, also, was "much disgusted and disturbed to see the Huron women eat the lice from themselves and their children; for they ate them as if they were both good and tasty."[4] The Montagnais practised a similar custom, stating that it was "not that they liked the taste of them, but because they want to bite those that bite them."[5]

Mollusca.

The various species of clams seem always to have been favourite articles of food among the Iroquois. This is borne out by the archæological evidence found on village sites identified as Iroquoian.[6] The genera include *Anodonta*, *Unio*, and *Margaritana*. A Cayuga name given was ga'nu'sa'. The same name is applied to oysters.

---

[1] Informant, Baptist Thomas, Onondaga Castle, N.Y.

[2] Loskiel, *Hist. of Mission*, pt. I, p. 66.

[3] *Jesuit Relations*, R. G. Thwaites ed., vol. XV, p. 163.

[4] Sagard, *Voyages*, vol. I, p. 76.

[5] *Jesuit Relations*, R. G. Thwaites ed., vol. VI, p. 245.

[6] Wintemberg, W. J., *The Use of Shells by the Ontario Indians*, Ont. Arch. Rep., 1907, pp. 38, 39.

The bivalves are boiled and made into soup. Milk, salt, and butter are frequently added.

Another method of cooking, according to Chief Gibson, is to fry them in butter or grease.

Various land and water gasteropoda were no doubt employed, particularly in times of scarcity. An Onondaga name for water gasteropods is dji'sǫ̌wǫ̌ (brains). This is also applied to the slugs or shell-less snails. An Onondaga name for shell-bearing gasteropoda is unǫsageⁿdɩ' (they carry a house). A Cayuga term is dri'drǫ'wa' (having horns).

Among the historical references to this class of foods is one by Loskiel, who mentions the employment of "mussels and oysters."[1]

Brickell also remarks of these that "they are only made use of by the Indians, who eat them after five or six hours boiling to make them tender."[2] According to the same writer, certain kinds were preserved by drying.[3]

SACCHARINE FOODS.

Maple Syrup and Sugar.

The sap of the maple, birch, and several other trees was employed prehistorically. Besides its use as a beverage, it was boiled and thickened somewhat, though its manufacture into sugar must have been exceedingly difficult, if not impossible, with the crude utensils at hand.

References to the employment of sap are found in several of the earlier Relations. Nouvel, for instance, refers to a "liquor that runs from the trees toward the end of Winter, and which is known as 'Maple-water.' "[4] This was written in 1671, and refers to the Ottawas of Ekaentouton. Le Jeune, in 1634, observed that the Montagnais, when pressed by famine, eat "the shavings or bark of a certain tree, which they call Michtan, which they split in the Spring to get from it a juice, sweet as

---

[1] Loskiel, *History*, pt. I, p. 66.

[2] Brickell, *History of North Carolina*, p. 249.

[3] Ibid., pp. 288, 367.

[4] *Jesuit Relations*, R. G. Thwaites ed., vol. LVI, p. 101.

honey or as sugar; . . . but they do not enjoy much of it, so scanty is the flow." Neither of the foregoing refer to sugar, mention of which occurs only in later records.

Carr, with regard to sugar-making, considers that "As to the maple sugar . . . there can be no doubt. It was made where-ever the tree grew, and it found especial favour as an ingredient in their preparation of parched corn-meal, or as we call it, nocake or rockahominy."[1] Charlevoix, on the other hand, states that the Abnaki, "when the sap begins to rise . . . make a Jag or Notch in the Trunk of the Maple, and by Means of a Bit of Wood which they fix in it, the Water runs as by a Spout. . . . It is certain that they did not know how to make a Sugar of it, which we have since taught them. They were contented to let it boil a little, to thicken it something, and make a Sort of Syrup."[2] The latter observation seems to have been true throughout the area occupied by the Iroquois and their neighbours, although, with improved utensils, the making of sugar was quickly adopted.

Methods, within the historical period, appear to have changed but little. Loskiel refers to the use of a "funnel made of bark" which was used to convey the sap into "wooden troughs or dishes." Basswood chips for spiles and wooden troughs are still employed by some of the Iroquois (Plate X). Troughs were also made of elm bark. A Cayuga informant[3] states that an old-time method of tapping was by breaking the end of a limb.

The sugar-moulds described by Loskiel were "broad, wooden dishes of about two inches in depth." The crystallizing syrup was "stirred about in these until cold." The sugar was also allowed to crystallize in the kettles.[4] A model of a box-like mould, held together by wooden clamps, was made for the writer by one of the older Onondaga.[5] According to the latter, the sugar was also run into small tin pans, forming cakes of a certain weight.

---

[1] Carr, *Food of Certain American Indians*.

[2] Charlevoix, *A Voyage to North America*, vol. I, p. 83.

[3] John Jamieson, jun.

[4] Loskiel, *History*, pt. I, pp. 72, 73.

[5] Peter John.

The sap was stored, in preparation for boiling, in a large wooden trough formed by hollowing out the trunk of a tree.

The hard or sugar maple (*Acer saccharinum*) was considered best, although the soft maple (*Acer saccharum*) and the birch were also used. Besides its food use, the sap of the soft maple is considered valuable for sore eyes. It was stated by a Cayuga[1] that hickory chips were sometimes boiled to obtain a "sweet water," which was added to corn to make corn soup. According to Charlevoix, the Abenaki also employed the sap of the plane or buttonwood, the ash, walnut trees of different sorts, and the wild cherry.[2] Walnut sap is said to have been very sweet, though the sugar made from the wild cherry is said never to have lost its bitterness. The use of "les Noyers," or nut-bearing trees, and the ash is confirmed by Lafitau, who remarks that the sap of the ash, though delicate, was scanty in flow.[3]

Terms used (Onondaga).

> Bark pot, ga'sọ˄da' gana˄djia'.
> Sap trough, niga·họ'wa'sɑ' ọ'gaieda'kwa'.
> Sap, uwɛnowɛ'da'gɛt' (sweet juice), or wa'gae'da'.
> Maple syrup, ohwa˄da' use'sda'.
> Maple sugar, ohwa˄da' uwɛnowɛ˄da' (or simply, uwe-nowɛ˄da').
> Spile, ọ'gaieda'kwa' o'ga'ɛ' (to stick in, chip).
> Gash made in the tree, ga'o˄.
> Sugar mould, eänawɛ'daa'kwa' gahọ˄sää' (to put sugar in, box or trough).
> Wooden storage trough for sap, t'negaa'kwa'.
> The sap is running, ga'ne'gu's.
> He is gathering the sap, hane'gai'ets.
> He is boiling the sap, hoyaha˄dọ'.
> They are boiling the sap, diuyä'hąs.
> He is making sugar, hainawɛ'do'niaha'.
> He is tapping the trees, ha'gaie'tha' (putting chips in the tree).

---

[1] John Jamieson, jun.
[2] Charlevoix, *A Voyage to North America*, pt. I, p. 84.
[3] Lafitau, *Moeurs des Sauvages Ameriquains*, pt. II, pp. 155, 156.

The tree is tapped, wa'ga'e'da'.

It is ready for sugaring, gondihe'do'niuŋk one (it is making bubbles of steam).

Season for sugar-making, undänada˄sänia˅ta' (fixing up the sugar camp).

Honey.

The honey-bee (*Apis mellifica*) was a European importation. Kalm, who visited the Iroquois country in 1748-50, remarks that "the Indians likewise generally declare, that their fathers had never seen any bees either in the woods or anywhere else, before the Europeans had been several years settled here. This is further confirmed by the name which the Indians give them: . . . they call them English flies. . . . They have not yet been found in the woods on the other side of the Blue Mountains, which confirms the opinion of their being brought to America of late."[1]

The honey used was principally that derived from escaped swarms, while the methods employed in locating these resemble those of the white settlers.

Bees in the act of swarming are stopped by throwing water upon them, or shooting near them.

When a bee-tree is chopped down, a little honey is left for the bees in order to secure "good luck;" otherwise a man is liable to have his game stolen by other animals, or to meet with other troubles.

The honey is cleared of dirt and leaves by hanging it up in a cotton bag to drain. Besides its use as a food, the honey is considered medicinal.

A remedy for bee stings is to obtain some clover leaves, mash them a little, and apply as a poultice. This appears to contain the idea of sympathetic magic, the clover being the favourite resort of bees.

---

[1] Kalm, *Travels*, vol. I, p. 288.

Some Onondaga Terms.

Honey-bee, gǫdiänäwą̈donia'ha' (making honey or sweet stuff).

Bumble bee, na'gǫda'gwa'ne'gona (big bee).

Honey, use'sda'.

BEVERAGES.

Water was naturally the most common beverage. The sites of villages everywhere are found to be in proximity to some sort of water supply. Sometimes this was in the form of springs, or spring creeks, rivers, or even pondholes or ditches, sources which are still more or less in favour in many localities.

When a red blood-sucker or leech (On., djiägwai'ı'nı' utgwę''da' nigaia'do''dä') is seen in the water, the latter is not considered fit for drinking. The people are warned by the longhouse preachers against water contaminated in this way and are told that it will cause them to waste away and die.[1]

Palisaded villages were frequently constructed so as to provide a water supply, though the unfortunate results of neglect in this respect were at times experienced.

One of the most easily prepared beverages was probably that noted by Loskiel, who remarks that "the common drink of the Indians at their meals is nothing but the broth of the meat they have boiled, or spring water."[2] He also observed that they "prepare a kind of liquor of dried bilberries, sugar and water, the taste of which is very agreeable to them." These were probably some one of several species of *Vaccinium* or blueberry, although the name is sometimes popularly applied to the juneberry, *Amelanchier canadensis*, and related species. The water in which corn bread is boiled is likewise preserved for drinking purposes.[3]

---

[1] John Echo and others, Grand River reserve.

[2] Loskiel, *Hist. of the Mission of the United Brethren*, pt. I, p. 74.

[3] A Seneca name given by Parker is O'niyustagi'. *N. Y. State Mus. Bull.*, 144, p. 71; cf. also Beverly, *Hist. and Present State of Virginia*, p. 151.

Jesuit Relations, R. G. Thwaites ed., vol. XV, p. 159: "The usual sauce with the food is pure water, juice of corn or of squashes."

Berries were evidently quite frequently used in the preparation of drinks. These were not only noted historically, but are popular at present. Blackberries or thimbleberries and water, sweetened with maple sugar, is common both for home consumption and in longhouse ceremonies. This drink was called ᴜhiaʹ-geꞇʹ (On.). The fresh berries are preferred when these are obtainable, though they are also dried or otherwise preserved and enjoyed throughout the winter. This drink is employed as a refreshment at the meetings called hadiʹhiʹdus and the making of nigaꞌneʹgaaꞌ medicine, as are also similar concoctions of strawberries and raspberries at their respective festivals. At certain of these functions the juice is sometimes sprayed from the mouth upon the heads of those desiring health and prosperity for the coming season.[1] In such cases the liquid must be made by those undergoing the ceremony. Huckleberries may be used for the same purpose. Fresh blackberries are particularly sought after for the Big Green Corn Dance in the early autumn. The drinkers in each case make an effort to get a share of the berries which settle to the bottom. An active medicinal value, aside from ceremonial uses, is ascribed to several varieties of berries and other fruits or to beverages made from them.

Corn coffee, made after the following method, is a well-known Iroquois beverage; whole ears of corn are dried, then placed on the coals and turned carefully until they roast. These are placed in a kettle of water and boiled. Sugar may be added if desired, also buttermilk or ordinary milk. A name applied to this by Chief Gibson is ganɇhageꞏiʹdaᵛwiꞌ dɇyǫtnegǫʹdą̈ꞌ, meaning "roasted corn to make a drink."

A sunflower coffee is said, by the same informant, to have been made by roasting sunflower seeds, grinding them a little in the mortar, sifting, and saving the shells. Boiling water poured over the latter is said to make a beverage tasting just like coffee. This was called ą̈yeditshäᵛniaꞌ (On.).

A so-called coffee was also stated to be sometimes made from the wild plum, gą̈häꞌhä. The plums are cut along one side, the stones removed, and the fruit dried on boards or in evaporating

[1] Boyle, Dr., *Ont. Arch. Rep., 1898*, p. 140.

baskets in the sun. The beverage is made by adding boiling water to the dried fruit and is called dặyụtne'gǫdặ' (On.).

The sweet juice derived from the stalks of corn is frequently mentioned by the early writers. Loskiel states with regard to this that the cornstalk "when unripe, is full of a sweet juice like sugar."[1] Some of the older people still remember when sections of cornstalk were cut and chewed as a means of allaying thirst.

Another coffee-like concoction, evidently known in Loskiel's time, was made from chestnuts. "Sometimes they are roasted like coffee-beans, and a kind of beverage made of them, nearly resembling coffee in color and taste, but of a laxative nature."[2]

Hickory nuts, still plentiful throughout the Iroquois country, formed the basis of a savory beverage. The writer previously quoted observes that "the Indians gather a great quantity of sweet hiccory nuts, which grow in great plenty in some years, and not only eat them raw, but extract a milky juice from them, which tastes well and is nourishing."[3]

A drink which was always welcomed in its appropriate season was the juice of the maple and sometimes of the birch.[4] All that was necessary was a rough incision in the bark or the broken end of an overhanging limb, with a dish of bark or wood to catch the liquid. Lafitau mentions, among sources of sugar or sap other than the maple, "les Noyers," members of the hickory and walnut family, whose juice, however, would seem to have been too strongly medicinal to have been generally in favour.[5]

Maple sap is said to have been sometimes fermented and used as an intoxicant, though its use could never have been at all common. This sometimes turned to a vinegar, which was

---

[1] Loskiel, pt. I, p. 67.

[2] Ibid., p. 70.

[3] Ibid., p. 71; cf. also Smith, *Map of Virginia*, 1612, p. 12.

[4] Hunter, J. D., *Memoirs* (London, 1824), p. 415.

[5] Williams, Roger, *Key*, p. 90: "Beere" drink is mentioned. This was made by the English settlers from the chips of the walnut, the idea probably being borrowed from the Indians. The drink was said to taste good and to be mildly laxative.

also consumed.[1] The fermentation of sweet liquids and fruit juices takes place so readily that the discovery could not have been readily avoided. The chief difficulty seems to have been in the lack of receptacles for keeping the beverages. In Pinkerton's voyages we find the assertion with regard to certain tribes inhabiting Virginia, not far from the Island of Roanoke, that "their drink is only water, but while the grape lasteth they drink wine, and for want of casks to keep it, all the year after they drink water, but it's sodden with ginger in it and black cinnamon, and sometimes sassafras, and divers other wholesome and medicinal herbs and trees."[2]

That wine-making was not an Iroquois custom is indicated by Lafitau, who observed that, "the grape is found in all parts of America; but it was nowhere cultivated by the savages, nor did they know the secret of making wine."[3] Sagard remarks the same of the Hurons.[4] Wine of wild grapes was given by a Caughnawaga informant[5] as an ingredient in a medical prescription for bloodlessness, though there is nothing to indicate any ancient origin.[6] Mohawk names for the wild grape are gar'sagų'ha' or o'nǫ'harɩ'.

Infusions of the leaves, roots, twigs, bark, or flowers of certain plants and trees were frequently employed and quite a number of the older people still remember their use. One of the best lists was furnished by Mrs. John Williams (Mo.), Caughnawaga:

Hemlock, onǫ'da'ųwɩ'. Take the leaves, steep, sweeten with maple sugar, and eat with corn bread or at meals. Other names are ganę'dęs (Ca.), sanądaʌta' (Ca.), wana'djų'ni' (Mo.).

---

[1] Fermented sap is called in Onondaga, gawi'shɩ' uwɛnawę'da'geɩ'. Vinegar is deyu'nega'hiyuʌdjis.

[2] Pinkerton, *Voyages and Travels*, vol. 12, p. 568.

[3] Lafitau, *Moeurs*, vol. I, p. 112.

[4] Sagard-Theodat, *Voyage*, vol. I, p. 71.
Hunter, J. D., *Memoirs* (London, 1824), p. 261.

[5] Mrs. Katie Dybeau.

[6] Lawson (per Brickell), *Nat. Hist. of N. Carolina*, p. 291: "Neither were they acquainted with any kind of intoxicating liquors before the arrival of Christians." These were neighbours of the Iroquois.

Black or sweet birch (*Betula lenta*), djo'djo'rǫ. The twigs from the small growth are taken, made into a small bundle, and steeped.

Sassafras, a'tsdas, was widely used. A tea was made of the roots. This was frequently employed at weddings on account of its agreeable odour. Loskiel states that sassafras "flowers serve for tea."[1] The tree was also highly valued for its medicinal virtues. A Cayuga name is wa'ă'nagras. This is rendered in Onondaga as u'ąna'gäs. A Cayuga name by J. Hess is na'statra'.

Spicewood, dawaaserų'ni, furnished its sweet-smelling twigs and branches which were cut up and steeped. Cayuga and Seneca names are dewatai'niäs and da⁻dia's.

The wintergreen, dzo'dzo'rųtsera'geras (Mo.).[2] was included. The leaves of this were steeped. It is called in Onondaga unä⁻dadę's.

Yarrow, deyohuda⁻sǫ, a plant which, like all the others named was used for medicine, or as a medicinal ingredient, formed a very agreeable drink when an infusion of suitable strength was made. Yarrow was also called aro'zǫ oda⁻sų, or squirrel tail. Onondaga names given are unę⁻da' and ga'sąhäyenda'-kwa' (looking like frosty or cold weather).

Witch-hazel, dagwa'a'dro'ni' (Ca.) was stated by Chief David Jack to be made into a decoction of suitable strength, sweetened with maple sugar and used as a tea at meals.

The young twigs of red raspberry, gwa⁻dänę' (Sen.), according to Barber Black, Tonawanda, N.Y., were stripped of the leaves, placed in hot water and steeped, then sweetened with sugar in the usual way.

Sumac seed clusters seem also to have been boiled, during the autumn and winter, as a beverage. It is probable that infusions of many other materials, including various edible roots, and forming broths or soups, with more or less of a food value,

---

[1] Loskiel, pt. I, p. 115.
Hunter, J. D., *Memoirs* (London, 1824), p. 420.
[2] This means. "It smells like black birch."

were used from time to time.[1] A suggestion of this is found in
the use by the Abenaki of the juice from the bruised roots of the
cat-tail and other plants. A variety of names are given for
sumac: utgoʳda' (On. and Mo.), na'ju'k (Ca.), utgodago'a
(Ca.), dji'tgwa niuha'do'dą (Ca.), dara'gwi (Mo.).

Monarda, horse-mint, or Oswego tea, as it is variously called,
Monarda fistulosa, represented the mint family, which suggests
that other mints may also have been pressed into service. Among
the more suitable for the purpose would be the peppermint,
spearmint, pennyroyal, and others. A Cayuga name for monarda is ganu'da'.

Even urine seems to have been used in cases of necessity,
such as forced marches. Seaver, for instance, notes that it was
offered to captives. According to the Relations, it was also
administered at times as a medicine.

It seems somewhat surprising that corn was not fermented.
The Zuñis, for instance, prepare a drink from sprouted corn.
This is claimed to be non-intoxicating. A drink is also made of
pop-corn, "ground in the finest mill. The powder is put into a
bowl and cold water is poured over it. The mixture is strained
before it is drunk. This beverage is also used in ceremonies and
during fasts of the rain priests."[2] An Iroquois food-drink
resembling the latter was made by parching corn, grinding it to
a flour in the wooden mortar, and mixing it with maple sugar.
This was used as a hunting or travelling food. A small wooden
dish was carried along and a small quantity of the flour mixed
with cold water and drunk as required. According to Thomas
Key (On.), a small cup was used for this purpose by the hunter,

---

[1] Slippery elm inner bark is often made into a mucilaginous decoction,
considered to have a food as well as a medicinal value. This was no doubt
familiar to the Iroquois.

[2] Stevenson, M. C., *The Zuñi Indians*, 23rd Ann. Rep. B. A. E., p. 369.

Adair describes a drink made of "their flinty corn," though in this case,
after pounding and sifting, they boiled the meal in large earthen pots, then
strained off the thinnest part, and diluted it with water for drinking. *Hist.
of the North American Indians*, p. 416.

In the Second Voyage of Sir John Hawkins, 1564, it is remarked of corn
meal that "it maketh also good beverage, sodden in water, and nourishable."
Hakluyut, *Voyages*, p. 46.

so that it would not cover his eyes, and no one else was allowed to drink from the same cup. A drink of the mixture was taken immediately upon leaving home.

The fresh blood of slaughtered animals was employed as a food or drink by a number of aboriginal races, but does not seem, aside from the alleged use of the blood of captives taken in war,[1] to have been particularly favoured by the Iroquois.

Grease, both in a solid and liquid condition, as well as various animal oils, were probably quite widely used. Historical references to their consumption by the Iroquois are found in the accounts of the early missionaries and others.[2]

The ability of the Indians to go without food or drink for long periods has been frequently remarked. Du Peron states of the Hurons that "as for drinks, they do not know what they are, —the sagamité serving as meat and drink; when not on their journeys, they will go six months without drinking."[3]

SALT AS A FOOD MATERIAL.

Salt was evidently adopted principally during the later historical period. Loskiel describes the Iroquois attitude towards salt by stating that "neither the Iroquois, Delaware, nor any in connexion with them, eat their meat raw, but frequently without salt, though they have it in abundance."[4] The fact that several old-time foods, such as corn bread, corn and bean soup, etc., are made without salt would also indicate that the usage is modern.

The existence of salt in New York state and in several places in western Ontario from Kincardine to Sarnia suggests that a special reason existed for its omission by the Iroquois. Historical references are unanimous in stating that salt was seldom or never used by nearly all the eastern Indians at or

---

[1] *Jesuit Relations*, R. G. Thwaites ed., vol. XLIV, p. 55.

[2] Ibid., vol. XLII, p. 65: Iroquois drink bear's grease. Cf. also Bartram, *Observations*, p. 25.

[3] *Jesuit Relations*, R. G. Thwaites ed., vol. XV, p. 163. Cf. also Chaumonot, *Autobiographie*, p. 56: "La soif ne se fait jamais senti, parceque nous ne mangeons rien de salé, et que la nourriture est toujours très liquide."

[4] Loskiel, *Hist. of the Mission of the United Brethren*, pt. I, p. 65.

immediately following the discovery. Cartier noted of the Indians met by him that "their entire living is without a taste of salt."[1] Charlevoix, Chaumonot, Carver, Jogues, Champlain, and various writers in the Relations refer to this apparent aversion to salt, both among the Iroquois and among the Algonkin tribes to the north and east of them.

Hoffman remarks that "Salt is not used by the Menomini during meals, neither does it appear to have a place in the kitchen for cooking or baking. Maple syrup is used instead, and it is singular how soon one may acquire the taste for this substitute for salt, even on meats."[2] Lafitau and others comment on the use of maple syrup and sugar in cookery.[3] The fact that no salt was used by the Montagnais is repeated again and again in the Relations.

The Mandans were found by Catlin to be non-users of salt, though their country abounded in the material.[4] Other Siouan tribes, such as the Omaha, collected the mineral for use. The Shawnee, unlike their more northern relatives, were famed as salt-makers.

A desire for some saline material was shown by certain tribes. The Cherokee, an Iroquoian tribe residing to the southwest, used lye, and salt is even yet seldom employed by the eastern division of the tribe. Beverly writes regarding the Indians of Virginia, that "they have no Salt among them, but for seasoning, used the Ashes of Hiccory, Stickweed, or some other Wood or Plant, affording a Salt ash."[5] Hariot also reports that "there is an hearbe which in Dutch is called Melden. Some of those that I describe it unto, take it to be a kind of Orage; it groweth about foure or five foote high: of the seede thereof they make a thick broth, and pottage of a very good taste: of the stalks by burning into ashes they make a kind of salt earth, wherewithall many use sometimes to season their brothes; other salte they knowe not."[6]

[1] Cartier, *Bref Récit*, p. 25.
[2] Hoffman, W. J., *The Menomini Indians*, 14th Ann. Rep. B.A.E., p. 286.
[3] Lafitau, *Moeurs*, vol. II, p. 157.
[4] Catlin, G., *Letters and Notes*, pp. 124, 125.
[5] Beverly, *The History and Present State of Virginia*, vol. III, p. 15.
[6] Hariot, *A briefe and true report*. Cf. also Lawson, *Nat. Hist. of North Carolina* (per Brickell), p. 401 and p. 340.

The Hurons, according to the Relations, sometimes "put in pieces of cinders, to season the sagamité,"[1] and used "no salt or other condiment" of this nature.

A possible explanation of the Iroquois non-use of salt may be, as suggested by Beauchamp, that their original habitat was in some area where salt was not readily obtained.[2] Some weight is added to this by the fact that neither the Eskimo nor the northern Algonkins favoured its use. The objections are still advanced by some of the older men on the various reservations that physical deterioration generally and such ailments as decay of the teeth and other complaints result from eating salt.

The Iroquois, in fact, seem to have retained this attitude as late as 1654. Marie de l'Incarnation, for instance, relates that the Iroquois supposed the water of a certain salt spring to be poison and thought that it was by a miracle that the French obtained salt from the water.[3] This is confirmed by an observation of the missionary le Moine that the Onondagas dared not drink of a salt spring which he visited, holding that there was an evil spirit in it which rendered it foul.[4]

The gradual adoption of salt is noted by a number of early writers. Even the Montagnais began eventually to use it, and the decreasing prejudice of the Iroquois is remarked by Conrad Weiser, who, about the year 1737, went with his host to see a salt spring from which the Indians boiled "handsome salt for use."

A later adaptation of the use of salt is probably to be found in certain medicinal uses. Loskiel cites the fact that "Salt has lately been found (1794) to be a powerful antidote (for rattle-

---

[1] *Jesuit Relations*, R. G. Thwaites ed., vol. XV, p. 163.

[2] Sagard-Theodat, *Voyages*, vol. I, p. 63, speaking of the Hurons, though apparently rather erroneously with regard to distance from salt springs, states that "we found ourselves very well while not eating salt, moreover we were nearly three hundred leagues from any salt waters. And upon my return to Canada (Quebec) I was ill from eating it at first, after having abstained from it so long; which makes me think that salt is not necessary to the preservation of life or health."

[3] Marie de l'Incarnation, *Lettres*, t. II, p. 64; quoted in *Jesuit Relations* R. G. Thwaites ed., vol. XLI, p. 256.

[4] *Jesuit Relations*, R. G. Thwaites ed., vol. XLI, pp. 123, 125.

snake bite); and if immediately applied to the wound, or dissolved in water and used as a lotion, no danger is to be feared."[1] It was also looked upon as a counteractant to witchcraft, the same writer remarking that "the Indians say that their poison and witchcraft has no effect upon white people, because they eat so much salt in their victuals."[2]

A salt remedy, obtained among the Cayugas of Brant county,[3] was claimed to be effective for "inflammation of the bowels." Salt is placed in the patient's hands and on the feet. A decoction of black cherry bark is administered internally, and a poultice of the boiled bark applied to the abdomen. An Onondaga remedy for a burn or scald is to apply wet salt.

An interesting taboo or restriction with regard to the use of salt is found everywhere in connexion with the ministrations of the Nega⌣ne′ga'a'[4] or Little Water Company. The patient who accepts their services and partakes of the medicine must be seen by no one for ten days but by an attendant, must eat only bread and cold water, and must abstain from all kinds of meat, salt, soda, etc. When the person becomes better, a white hen, white beans, rice, corn soup, a pig's head or other white-coloured article of food must be prepared, after which the restrictions are removed.[5]

Young people of both sexes at puberty, according to an Oneida informant,[6] were formerly made to live in a shanty in the bush, with no fire and only one blanket. They were obliged to go in swimming, no matter how cold, and to engage in exercises for warmth. They would stay there for nearly a month. Boys were not allowed to eat anything hot at the time the voice changed, also no salt, pepper, or other materials of the kind. This was said to make the teeth good.

[1] Loskiel, *Hist. of the Mission of the United Brethren*, pt. I, p. 114.
[2] Ibid., p. 119.
[3] Mrs. Peter Atkins (Ca.), informant.
[4] Onondaga name. This taboo is briefly noted by Adair, *A Hist. of the American Indians*, p. 125.
[5] Chief Alex. Hill.
[6] Anthony Day.

Small bottles or receptacles for salt were formerly woven from the dried husks of corn and are still sometimes made by the older people. An Onondaga name given for these is unuya' gätsιⁿda' (Plate XXXI, figs. d, e).

Names for Salt.

> Onondaga—udjikeᵥ'da'.
> Mohawk—deyuhio'djis.
> Oneida—onǫda'gelᶜ (said to be for onǫda'geli').
> Cayuga—djιke'da'.
> Seneca—odji'ke'da'.

BIBLIOGRAPHY.

Adair, James.—History of the American Indians, London, 1775.

American Anthropologist.

American Folk-Lore, Journal of.

Bartram, John.—Observations made by, in his journey from Pennsylvania to Onondago, Oswego and the Lake Ontario in Canada, London, 1751.

Beauchamp, W. M.—New York State Museum Bulletin 41.

Beverly, Robert.—The history and present State of Virginia, London, 1705.

Boyle, Dr. David.—Ontario Archæological reports.

Brickell, John.—The natural history of North Carolina (from Lawson), ed. Dublin, 1737.

Brinton, D. G.—Myths of the New World, New York, 1868.

Bruyas.—Radices Verborum Iroquaeorum, J. M. Shea ed., Neo-Eboraci, 1863.

Carr, Lucien.—The food of certain American Indians and their methods of preparing it, American Antiquarian Society proceedings, 1895, N. S. Vol. X.

Carr, Lucien.—The mounds of the Mississippi valley, Smithsonian report, 1891.

Cartier, Jacques.—Bref Récit et Succincte Narration, etc. (1535-36), Tross ed., Paris, 1863.

Carver, Jonathan.—Travels through the interior parts of North America, London, 1778.

Caswell, Mrs. H. S.—Our life among the Iroquois Indians, Boston, 1892.

Champlain, Samuel de—Voyages of, Prince Society ed., Boston, 1878-1882.

Charlevoix, Pierre F. X. de.—A voyage to North America, Dublin, 1766.

Chaumonot, Pierre J. M.—Un Missionaire des Hurons (autobiography), Paris, 1885.

Coyne, Jas. H., ed.—Galinée's narrative, Ontario Historical Society papers and records, 1903.

156

De Candolle, A. L. P., Origin of Cultivated Plants, London, 1909.

Darwin, Charles.—Varieties of plants and animals under domestication, Vol. I, New York, 1900.

East, E. M.—A note concerning inheritance in sweet corn, Science, N. S., Vol. XXIX.

East (E. M.) and Hayes.—Inheritance in maize, Bulletin 167, Agricultural Experiment Station, New Haven, Conn.

Gilmore, M. R.—The aboriginal geography of the Nebraska country, Proceedings of the Mississippi Valley Historical Society, Vol. VI.

Handbook of American Indians, Bureau of American Ethnology, Washington, D.C.

Hariot, Thomas.—A Briefe and true report of the new found land of Virginia, 1585-86, London, 1900.

Harrington, M. R.—Some Seneca corn foods and their preparation, American Anthropologist, N. S., Vol. X, 1908.

Harshberger, J. W.—Cyclopedia of American agriculture, Vol. II.

Heckewelder, Jno. G. E.—History, manners, and customs of the Indian nations which formerly inhabited Pennsylvania and the neighbouring states, from translation by Du Ponceau, Paris, 1822.

Hennepin, Louis.—A new discovery of a vast country in America, ed. by R. G. Thwaites, Chicago, 1903.

Henry, Alex.—Travels and adventures in Canada and the Indian territories between the years 1760-1776, ed. by Jas. Bain, Toronto, 1901.

Hunter, J. D.—Memoirs of a captivity among the Indians of North America, London, 1824.

Jarvis, C. D.—American varieties of beans, Cornell University Bulletin 260.

Jesuit Relations, The, R. G. Thwaites ed.

Josselyn, Jno.—An account of two voyages to New England made during the years 1638-1663, Boston, 1865.

Josselyn, Jno.—New England's rarities discovered, London, 1672.

Kalm, Peter.—Travels into North America, London, 1771.

Lafitau, Jos. François.—Moeurs des Sauvages Ameriquains, Paris. 1724.

Lescarbot, Marc.—The History of New France, Paris, 1612.

Loskiel, G. H.—History of the mission of the United Brethren among the Indians in North America, London, 1794, translation by La Trobe.

Mooney, Jas.—Ghost dance religion, 14th Annual Report of the Bureau of American Ethnology.

Morgan, L. H.—League of the Ho-de-no-sau-nee or Iroquois, New York, 1904.

Morgan, L. H.—Houses and house life of the American aborigines, Washington, D. C., 1881.

Norton, A. T.—History of Sullivan's campaign, Lima, N.Y., 1879.

Parker, A. C.—Iroquois uses of maize and other food plants, New York State Educational Department Bulletin 482 (Museum Bulletin 144).

Parker, A. C.—The code of Handsome Lake, New York State Educational Department Bulletin 530 (Museum Bulletin 163).

Pinkerton, John.—A general collection of. . . voyages and travels in all parts of the world, London, 1808-14.

Russel, F.—The Pima Indians, 26th Annual Report of the Bureau of American Ethnology.

Sagard-Theodat.—Le Grand Voyage du Pays des Hurons, Tross ed., Paris, 1865.

Schoolcraft, H. R.—Information respecting the history, condition, and prospects of the Indian tribes of the United States, Archives of Aboriginal Knowledge, Vol. V, part I, Philadelphia, 1855.

Seaver, James E.—A narrative of the life of Mrs. Mary Jemison, printed for R. Parkin, London, 1826.

Shea, J. G. ed.—French-Onondaga dictionary (of 17th century), New York, 1859.

Shea, J. G. ed.—Life of Jogues (by Martin), New York, 1885.

Smith, Mrs. E. A.—Myths of the Iroquois, 2nd Annual Report of the Bureau of American Ethnology.

Sturtevant, E. L.—Kitchen garden esculents of American origin. American Naturalist. Vol. XIX.

Sturtevant, E. L.—History of garden vegetables, American Naturalist, Vol. XXIII.

Van der Donck.—New Netherlands (1656), New York Historical Society Transactions, series 2, Vol. I.

Western Reserve Historical Society Tracts, No. 64.

Williams, Roger.—A key into the language of America, collections of the Rhode Island Historical Society, Providence, 1827.

Wintemberg, W. J.—The use of shell by the Ontario Indians, Ontario Archæological Report, 1907.

Wissler, Clark.—The North American Indians of the Plains, Popular Science Monthly, May, 1913.

Wood, Wm.—New England's Prospect, Prince Society ed., Boston, 1865.

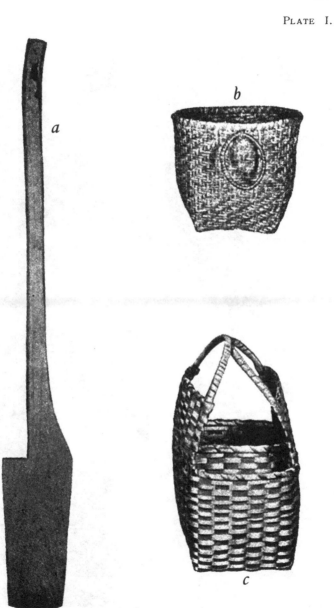

a. Digging stick, made by Peter John, On. Actual length about 40
inches. b. Corn washing basket of basswood inner bark. c. Planting
basket with compartments for carrying seeds which are to be planted
together, such as corn and beans. Division of Anthropology, Museum
Nos. III I. 900. 1010. 890. Collected by F. W Waugh at Grand River

PLATE II.

Longhouse, Oneidatown, Ontario.   (Page 12.)

PLATE III.

A.

A. Onondagá longhouse, Grand River reserve, Ontario.
B. Lower Cayuga longhouse, Grand River reserve.
The small building at the back in each is the cook-house, where the food is prepared for use in ceremonies. The cook-house in A was the old long-house. (Page 12.)

PLATE IV.

Model of ancient Iroquois house of elm bark. Division of Anthropology, Museum No. III I, 844. Collected by E. Sapir, Grand River reserve. (Page 39.)

PLATE V.

Harvesting scene. Husking the corn and braiding it into strings. From a sketch by Peter John, Onondaga, Grand River reserve. (Page 39.)

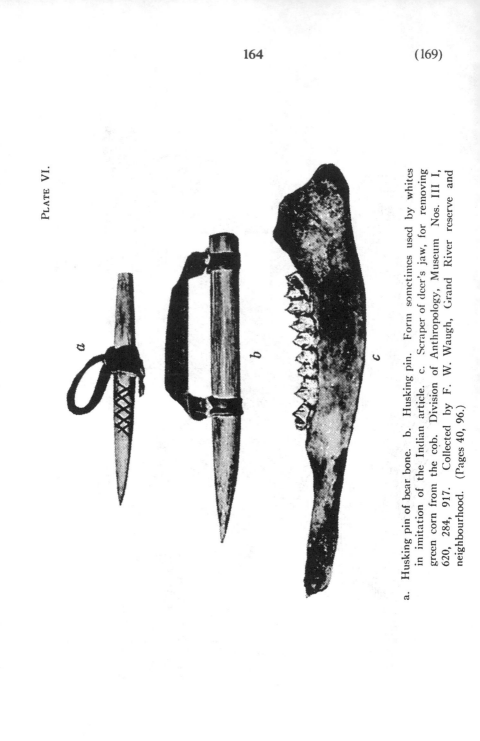

PLATE VI.

a. Husking pin of bear bone. b. Husking pin. Form sometimes used by whites in imitation of the Indian article. c. Scraper of deer's jaw, for removing green corn from the cob. Division of Anthropology, Museum Nos. III I, 620, 284, 917. Collected by F. W. Waugh, Grand River reserve and neighbourhood. (Pages 40, 96.)

PLATE VII.

Corn crib, Grand River reserve, Ontario. (Page 41.)

PLATE VIII.

Corn crib, farm of Daniel Winnie, Grand River reserve.   (Page 41.)

PLATE IX

Corn crib of poles, farm of Jacob Schuyler, Oneidatown, Ontario. (Page 41.)

PLATE X.

A.

A. Winter caches or pits for vegetables, Grand River reserve. (Page 43.)
B. Method of tapping trees, same locality.   (Page 141.)

PLATE XI.

Log houses of this kind, made like those of the early settlers, are quite common. These have practically no aboriginal features. A pine or other tree is often left for shade. Grand River reserve. (Page 49.)

Plate XII.

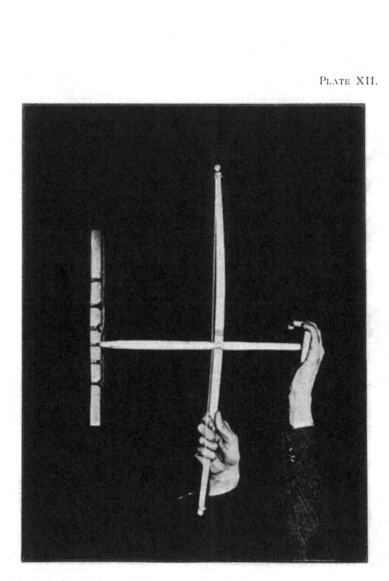

Method of using bow drill in fire-making by friction. Division of Anthropology, Museum No. III I, 764. Collected by F. W. Waugh at Tonawanda reserve, N.Y. (Page 50.)

Plate XIII.

Robert Smoke, Cayuga, Grand River reserve, using pump drill for fire-making. Division of Anthropology, Museum No. III I, 583. Collected by F. W. Waugh. (Page 52.)

PLATE XIV.

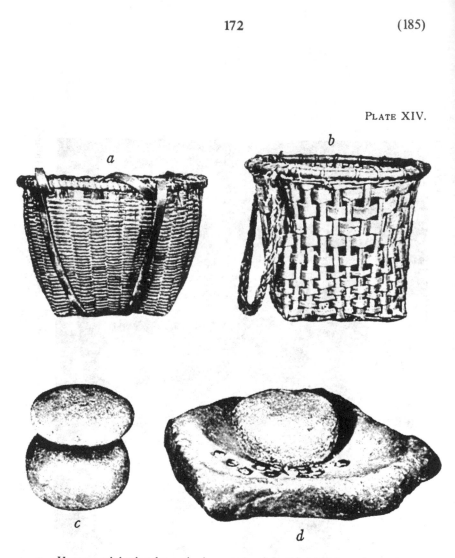

a.   Heavy pack basket for gathering wood.   Actual height of specimen about
one foot.   b.   Pack basket made from bark of young hickories.   c.
Stones used in cracking corn or nuts.   d.   Muller and mealing slab for
corn grinding, as used prehistorically and up to quite recent times.   Division of Anthropology, Museum Nos. III I, 722, 892, 740 a, b; VIII F,
5087.   a and c collected by F. W. Waugh at Caughnawaga, Quebec;
b collected at Grand River reserve.   (Pages 54, 59, 61.)

PLATE XV.

Mrs. John Williams, Mohawk, of Caughnawaga, using mealing stones. This method is still remembered by some of the older people and was occasionally used up to a generation or two ago. The bowl is made of maple knot. (Pages 60, 64, 65.)

PLATE XVI.

Shell corn in preparation for hulling and grinding, at Six Nations reserve. (Page 80.)

PLATE XVII.

Washing the corn to remove the hulls, after it has been boiled in wood ashes or lye, at Grand River reserve. (Page 80.)

PLATE XVIII

Grinding corn with wooden mortar and pestles at Grand River reserve. This is the method in general use on Iroquois reserves. (Page 58.)

PLATE XIX.

Sifting the meal after it has been ground in the mortar at Grand River reserve. The sifter being used is a "store" sieve. (Page 80.)

PLATE XX.

Method of carrying pack basket; the tump-line is of basswood inner bark; taken at Grand River reserve. (Page 61.)

PLATE XXI.

Pack basket used by Oneidas of Oneidatown, Ontario. Chief David Williams, wife and niece. Division of Anthropology, Museum No. III I, 834. Collected by F. W. Waugh, from Mrs. Henry

PLATE XXII.

a, c, d. Corn washing baskets, showing different styles of handle. Twilled
weave. b. Flexible washing basket made of basswood inner bark.
e. Pack basket for gathering corn. Actual height 16¼ inches. Division
of Anthropology, Museum Nos. III I, 206, 719, 891 a, 891 b, 342 a.
a, c, and d collected by F. W. Waugh at Grand River reserve; b at
Caughnawaga; e collected at Grand River reserve, per Chief John
Gibson. (Pages 39, 61, 62.)

PLATE XXIII

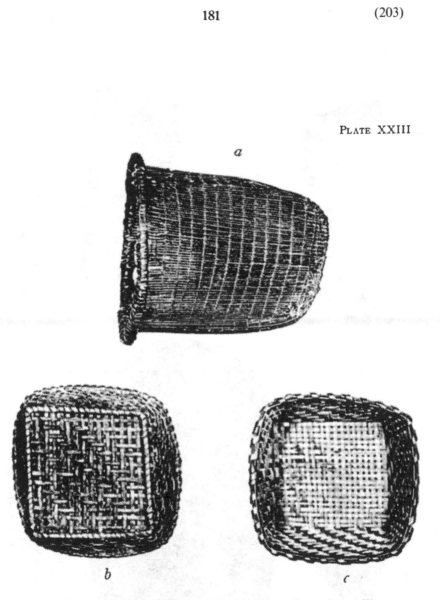

a. An old form of sifting basket, made of hickory splints. b, c. The ordinary form of sifting basket or sieve, made of black ash splints. Actual
width about 10 inches. Division of Anthropology, Museum Nos. III I,
721, 505, 271. a, collected at Caughnawaga by F. W. Waugh; b, collected at Seneca reserve, Oklahoma, by C. M. Barbeau; c, collected at
Grand River reserve, by F. W. Waugh. (Pages 63, 64.)

182

(205)

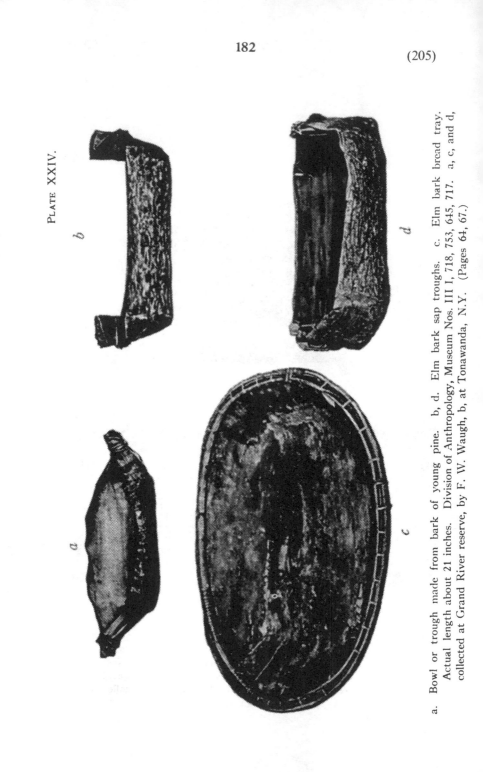

PLATE XXIV.

a. Bowl or trough made from bark of young pine. b, d. Elm bark sap troughs. c. Elm bark bread tray. Actual length about 21 inches. Division of Anthropology, Museum Nos. III I, 718, 753, 645, 717. a, c, and d, collected at Grand River reserve, by F. W. Waugh, b, at Tonawanda, N.Y. (Pages 64, 67.)

Plate XXV.

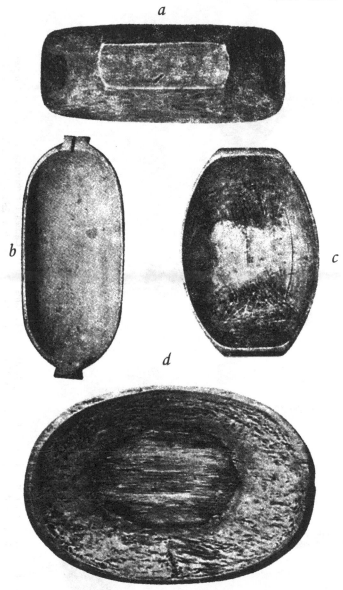

Bowls for bread-making and other household purposes. a is of beech, b and
d of basswood, and c of maple. Obtained from Grand River reserve.
Actual length of large bowl (d) about 2 feet, 4 inches. Division of
Anthropology, Museum Nos. III I, 96, 621, 339, 338. a, collected by
E. Sapir; b, by F. W. Waugh; c and d per Chief John Gibson. (Page
66.)

184 (209)

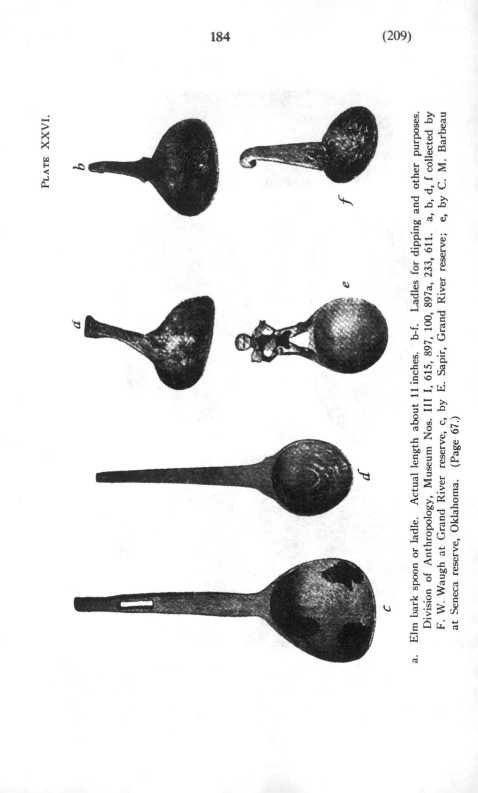

Plate XXVI.

a. Elm bark spoon or ladle. Actual length about 11 inches. b–f. Ladles for dipping and other purposes. Division of Anthropology, Museum Nos. III I, 615, 897, 100, 897a, 233, 611. a, b, d, f collected by F. W. Waugh at Grand River reserve, c, by E. Sapir, Grand River reserve; e, by C. M. Barbeau at Seneca reserve, Oklahoma. (Page 67.)

PLATE XXVII

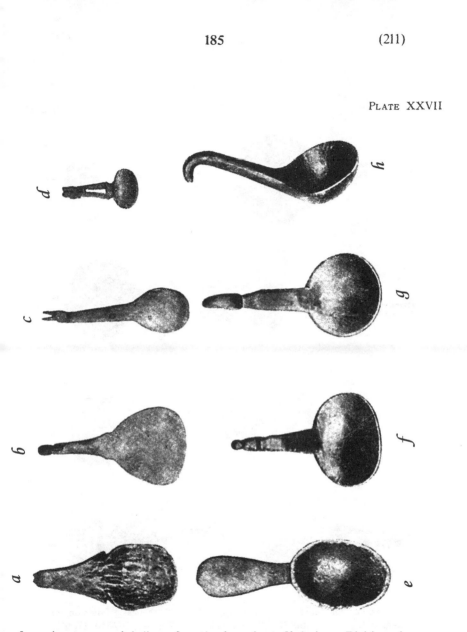

Iroquois spoons and ladles. Length of a, about 5½ inches. Division of Anthropology, Museum Nos. III I, 736, 273, 735, 359 a, 354, 360, 757, 796. a, c, collected by F. W. Waugh at Caughnawaga; b, d, e, f, per John Gibson, Grand River reserve; g, by F. W. Waugh at Tonawanda, N.Y.; h, by F. W. Waugh at Oneidatown, Ontario. (Page 67.)

PLATE XXVIII

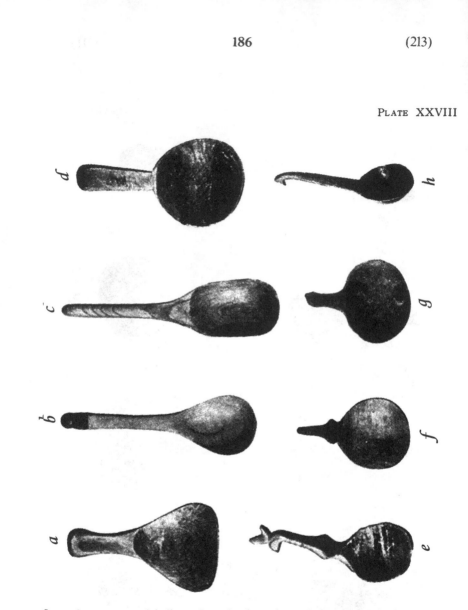

Iroquois spoons and ladles. Length of a, about 8 inches. Division of
Anthropology, Museum Nos. III I, 274, 428, 786, 429, 16, 610, 17, 613.
a, collected per Chief J. Gibson; b, d, by A. A. Goldenweiser at Grand
River reserve; c, by F. W. Waugh at Onondaga Castle, N.Y.; e, by
M. R. Harrington at Grand River reserve; f, h, by F. W. Waugh
at Grand River reserve; g, by M. R. Harrington at Cattaraugus,
N.Y. (Page 67.)

PLATE XXIX

Bread and stirring paddles. Length of a, 22¾ inches. Division of Anthropology, Museum Nos. III I, 756, 785, 49, 223, 18, 359 b. a, b, collected by F. W. Waugh at Tonawanda and Onondaga Castle respectively; c, by E. Sapir at Grand River reserve; d, by C. M. Barbeau at Seneca reserve, Oklahoma; e, by M. R. Harrington at Oneida reserve; f, per Chief J. Gibson, Grand River reserve. (Page 70.)

PLATE XXX

Bread paddles. Length of a, 30 inches. Division of Anthropology, Museum Nos. III I, 287, 899, 424, 898, 353, 352. a, b, d, collected by F. W. Waugh at Grand River reserve; c, by C. M. Barbeau at Seneca reserve, Oklahoma; e, f, per Chief J. Gibson, Grand River reserve. (Page 70.)

PLATE XXXI.

a. Knife of elm bark, used for skinning and other purposes. Actual length
about 9 inches. b. Knife made from scale of hickory bark. c. Knife-
like implement of flint. d. Corn-husk basket of a type frequently
used for holding salt for table use. e. Corn-husk bottle for salt. Actual
height, $3\frac{3}{4}$ inches. Division of Anthropology, Museum Nos. III I,
1012, 1011, 1028, 79 b, 80. a, b, collected by F. W. Waugh at Grand
River; c, collected by F. W. Waugh at Onondaga Castle, N.Y.; d, e,
by E. Sapir at Grand River. (Pages 71, 154.)

PLATE XXXII.

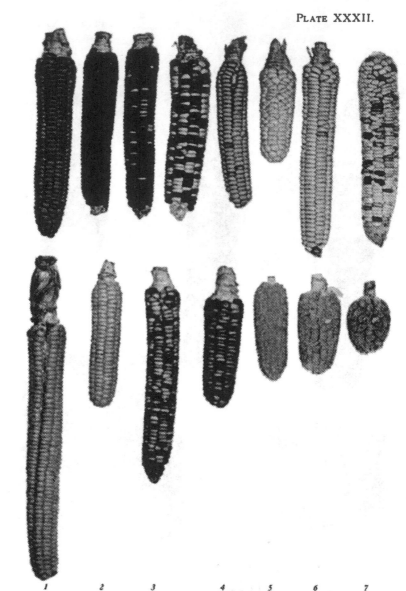

Some Iroquois corn varieties. Division of Anthropology, Museum Nos (beginning at upper left-hand corner) III I, 623, 294, 265, 627, 624 296, 295; III H, 138 a; III I, 622, 292 b, 298 a, 298 b, 835, 835 a, 835 b a 1-7 and b 1-4 collected by F. W. Waugh at Grand River reserve; b 5-7 at Oneidatown, Ontario; a 8 is a variegated dent corn collected by C. M Barbeau at Wyandotte, Oklahoma. It is also cultivated by the Iro quois. (Pages 75, 76.)

PLATE XXXIII.

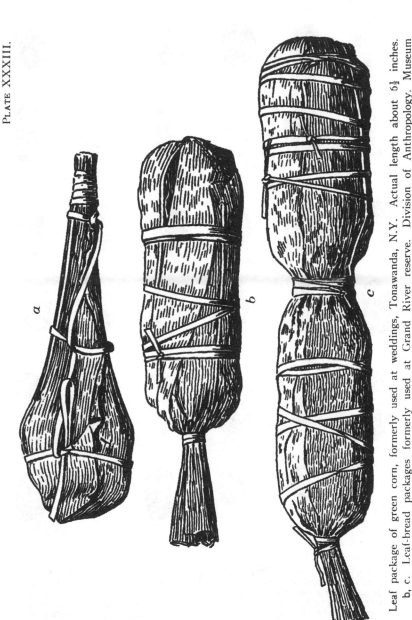

a. Leaf package of green corn, formerly used at weddings, Tonawanda, N.Y. Actual length about $6\frac{1}{2}$ inches. b, c. Leaf-bread packages formerly used at Grand River reserve. Division of Anthropology, Museum Nos. III I, 782, 916 a, 916 b. Collected by F. W. Waugh. (Page5 86, 87.)

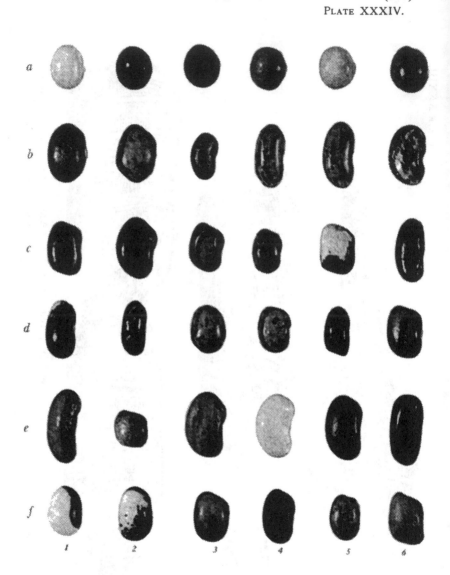

Iroquois bean varieties: e 6, Purple Flageolet; f 1, Yellow Eye; f 2, Golden Wax, probably a hybrid of. Division of Anthropology, Museum Nos. (beginning at upper left-hand corner) III I, 318, 972, 312, 306, 317, 299, 969, 971, 958, 977, 978, 942, 967, 964, 316, 965, 941, 950, 940, 949, 968, 960, 943, 303, 944, 545, 955, 946, 956, 301, 945, 315, 961, 937, 966, 314. e 2, collected by C. M. Barbeau at Seneca reserve, Oklahoma. The remainder collected by F. W. Waugh, a 1-6, b 1-3, c 2, c 3, d 2, d 6, e 1, e 3, e 4, e 6, f 2, f 4-6 at Grand River reserve; b 4-6, c 1, c 4-6, d 1, d 3, d 4, e 5, f 1, f 3 at Oneida town, Ontario; d 5, at Tonawanda, N.Y. (Pages 103, 105, 106, 107.)

PLATE XXXV.

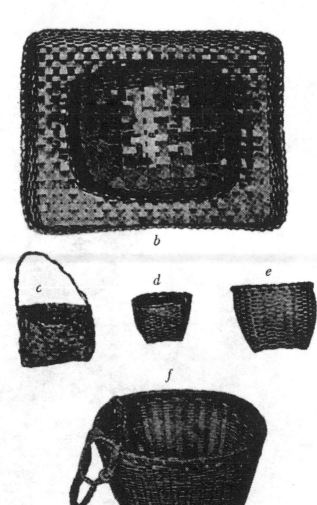

a, b. Baskets for drying berries or green corn. c, d, e. Berry-picking baskets for attaching to the belt. f. Pack basket for carrying berries Division of Anthropology, Museum Nos. III I, 751, 632, 487, 749, 748 893. a, e, d, collected by F. W. Waugh at Tonawanda, N.Y.; b, collected by F. W. Waugh at Grand River reserve; c, collected by C. M Barbeau at Seneca reserve, Oklahoma. (Pages 96, 126.)

PLATE XXXVI.

Method of carrying game or provisions on pack frame. Chief David Jack, Cayuga, Grand River reserve. (Page 131.)

PLATE XXXVII.

Elm bark toboggan for carrying game or provisions. John Jamieson, jun., Grand River reserve. (Page 131.)

PLATE XXXVIII.

Spearing fish with wooden spear. John Jamieson, jun., Grand River reserve. (Page 136.)

(235)

Plate XXXIX.

Fish-trap and dam.   Grand River reserve.   (Page 136.)